BIG ENGLISH 2 PLUS

Contents

Pearson Education Limited
Edinburgh Gate
Harlow
Essex CM20 2JE
England
and Associated Companies throughout the world.

www.pearsonelt.com/bigenglish

Authorised adaptation from the United States edition entitled Big English, 1st Edition, by Mario Herrera and Christopher Sol Cruz. Published by Pearson Education Inc. © 2013 by Pearson Education, Inc.

The right of Mario Herrera and Christopher Sol Cruz to be identified as the authors of this Work have been asserted by them in accordance with the Copyright, Designs and Patents Act 1988.

First published 2015

ISBN: 978-1-4479-8933-2

Set in Heinemann Roman
Editorial and project management by hyphen S.A.

Acknowledgements

The publisher would like to thank the following for their kind permission to reproduce their photographs:

(Key: b-bottom; c-centre; l-left; r-right; t-top)

123RF.com: captblack76 123b, jreika 126c, Pratchaya Leelapatchayanont 112c, lsaloni 126t, maxaltamor 35tc, Neven Milinković 54br, patrickhastings 126b, romasph 97 (d), viewstock 82l, Cathy Yeulet 82tr; **Alamy Images:** ableimages 75tr, 86t, 139bl, Aflo Co. Ltd 123tc, ARGO Images 51t/3, Asia Images Group Pte Ltd 107tl, Blend Images 60 (pilot), 72/5, Steve Bly 68r, Joerg Boethling 38br, Danita Delimont 24c, F1online digitale Bildagentur GmbH 56t, Glow Asia RF 138r/3, Jeff Greenberg 3bl, 17bl, 28br, Peter Grumann 10br, Hemis 51bl, imageBROKER 54bl, KidStock 102tl, Martin Wilson 123bc, Bob Masters 35tl, myLAM 123t, Nikreates 97 (c), Graham Oliver 46 (f), Pawel Libera Images 35br, PhotoAlto 102bl, Purepix 24r, Radius Images 51t/2, 59t, Alex Segre 54tr, Uwe Umstatter 94bl, 102bc, VStock 5t (a), Zak Waters 70t, Gari Wyn Williams 51t/4; **Corbis:** David Bathgate 10tl, Margaret Courtney-Clarke 24l, dpa / Jan Haas 56c, Reuters / Supri 38bl; **Datacraft Co Ltd:** 56b; **DK Images:** Max Alexander 51t/1, Lucy Claxton 131bl, Andy Crawford 79tl, Vanessa Davies 3tl, 9br, Steve Gorton 5b (e), 18l, 20/1 (b), 43tl, Britta Jaschinski 46 (a), Tim Ridley 66cl, 90/5, Rough Guides / Martin Richardson 51cl, 59b, 110tr, Rough Guides / Tim Draper 104l, William Shaw 91br, 100tl, Lorenzo Vecchia 98tr, 98br; **Eyewire:** 16 (c), 20/2 (a), 23br, 28tr, 135t; **FLPA Images of Nature:** David Hosking 114br; **Fotolia.com:** apops 65c, Andrey Bandurenko 43tr, dasharosato 51cr, dekanaryas 82br, f9photos 79tr, fotoperle 16 (f), 23tl, 135cr, Jose Manuel Gelpi 43bl, goodluz 60bl, Ilike 3br, 6br, 9tr, 134tl, Michael Ireland 26bc, Eric Isselée 110tl, Juulijs 5b (c), Jakub Krechowicz 90/4, 91cr, 93/3 (b), 103cl, krsmanovic 46 (b), Pavel Losevsky 46 (e), Lucky Dragon 26tc, Monkey Business 17br, 26b, moodboard 128tl, motorlka 90/8, 93/3 (a), 100bl, Natika 95br, Moreno Novello 10bl, Tyler Olson 60 (vet), 72/6, picsfive 95bc, 97 (h), primopiano 91tl, 97 (g), 103r, r-o-x-o-r 51br, RT Images 34tr, 35bl, 36bc, RTimages 16 (b), 19br, 20/1 (a), 23bl, RusGri 91bl, 93/4 (b), 100tc, Michael Shake 43br, 66r, shutswis 35tr, snaptitude 138r/2, sumnersgraphicsinc 18c, 20/3 (b), sveta 34tl, tropper2000 100bc, Tom Wang 138r/1, Ivonne Wierink 53cr, 90/11, Monika Wisniewska 70b, yanlev 16 (a), 28bl; **Getty Images:** David Page Photography 94tc, Diane Collins and Jordan Hollender 5t (c), 134tc, Gage 10tr, Katy McDonnell 3tr, 6tc, Juan Silva 40c, Damir Spanic 60 (actor); **Glow Images:** Ron Chapple 128br; **Pearson Education Ltd:** 18r, 20/3 (a), 63bl, 138l/3, Naki Kouyioumtzis 46 (c), Jules Selmes 6bl, 9bl, 138r/4, Studio 8 107br; **Shutterstock.com:** Africa Studio 98tl, Andrjuss 90/3, 97 (e), Andy Dean Photography 60 (doctor), 66cr, 72/4, Apples Eyes Studio 70bc, Yuri Arcurs 63tl, 138l/4, Nick Berrisford 109bl, Dean Bertoncelj 65l, Andre Blais 26t, Mark Bonham 72/3, Willyam Bradberry 109br, Diego Cervo 75tl, 139tl, Jacek Chabraszewski 94bc, cycreation 59bc, davegkugler 114bl, Elnur 72/8, eurobanks 95tc, Zadiraka Evgenii 5b (d), Iakov Filimonov 105b, Stephanie Frey 40r, Diane Garcia 68tl, Gemenacom 36b, Warren Goldswain 75br, 86c, 139tr, Goodluz 65r, Skazka Grez 95tl, Shawn Hempel 114tl, Jiri Hera 95bl, Horiyan 97 (a), Chris Howey 54tl, idiz 105t, irin k 5b (a), 7 (pencil), Tischenko Irina 131tl, Christopher Jones 60 (artist), 72/1, JonMilnes 68bl, Julian W 112r, Evgeny Karandaev 34bl, Karkas 36tc, 53cl, kkammphoto008 38tl, Serhiy Kobyakov 6tr, 134tr, Christopher Kolaczan 109tl, Vladimir Koletic 60 (singer), 66l, 72/7, Vitaly Korovin 90/6, 91cl, 103l, Kzenon 21 (a), Lucky Business 5t (b), Bruce MacQueen 109tr, Viktar Malyshchyts 53l, 90/10, 91tr, 93/1 (b), Rob Marmion 17tl, 21 (c), 63tr, 138l/2, mexrix 90/12, 93/4 (a), Dudarev Mikhail 131tr, Monkey Business Images 9tl, 21 (b), 90bl, 107cr, 107bl, 135cl, Morgan Lane Photography 6tl, 134b, Cora Mueller 16 (d), 19cr, 23tr, 135c, Dmitry Naumov 17tr, 19cl, 28tl, 128bl, Naypong 104cr, 117c, odze 90/9, 93/2 (b), 97 (f), 103cr, Presniakov Oleksandr 79br, P72 97 (b), 100tr, Panco 102tr, Perig 20/2 (b), 20/4 (b), Csaba Peterdi 16 (e), 19tl, 20/4 (a), 128tr, Stu Porter 141, Mike Price 110br, rickyd 104cl, riekephotos 40l, Alexander Ryabintsev 59tc, Sarunyu_foto 102tc, SergiyN 107tr, Rohit Seth 63cr, 138l/1, Dmitriy Shironosov 72/2, Victor Shova 105tc, 117l, sixninepixels 36t, Slaven 70tc, Smit 74, 78, Ljupco Smokovski 90/7, 93/1 (a), Bryan Solomon 95tr, James Steidl 35bc, STILLFX 7 (pen), Sam Strickler 112l, Ronald Summers 5b (f), 7 (football), 53r, Tatuasha 34br, Leah-Anne Thompson 75bl, 86b, 139br, Visionsi 60br, 138bl, Valentyn Volkov 5b (b), 7 (apple), 90/2, 98bl, Tatyana Vyc 90/1, 93/2 (a), 100br, wavebreakmedia 135bl, Peter Wey 131br, worldswildlifewonders 105bc, YapAhock 104r, 110bl, 117r, Zigroup-Creations 38tr, zimmytws 21 (d), ZouZou 94br, 102br; **SuperStock:** Biosphoto 114tr, Blend Images 29, 107cl, DeAgostini 79bl, Exactostock 21t, SuperFusion / Yuri Arcurs Media 94t; **www.imagesource.com:** photolibrary.com 46 (d)

Cover images: *Front:* **Shutterstock.com:** Iakov Filimonov l, Dudarev Mikhail c, stockyimages r

All other images © Pearson Education

Every effort has been made to trace the copyright holders and we apologise in advance for any unintentional omissions. We would be pleased to insert the appropriate acknowledgement in any subsequent edition of this publication.

Illustrated by
Robin Boyer, Zaharias Papadopoulos (hyphen), Jose Rubio, Christos Skaltsas (hyphen), Julia Wolf and Q2A Media Services.

In My Classroom

1 Listen and number.

2 Look at 1. Circle.

1 They're **coloring / counting**.

2 She's **writing / playing a game**.

3 They're **using the computer / listening**.

4 She's **gluing / counting**.

5 He's **writing / using the computer**.

6 He's **cutting / watching a DVD**.

3 Listen and sing. Then match and write.

a

b

c

d

Here's My Classroom!

Look! Here's my classroom.
And here are my friends!
Peter, Sarah, and Timothy,
Penny, Jack, and Jen!

Peter is cutting paper.
Penny is writing her name.
Sarah is listening to a story,
And Jack is playing a game.

Timothy is counting.
Jen is gluing.
We have fun and learn a lot.
What are your friends doing?

4 Draw your classroom. Then say.

5 Read and write.

1 How many Marias are there in the class?

There are ________________ Marias.

2 What is one Maria doing?

She's ____________________ and

______________________________.

3 What is the other Maria doing?

She's _______________________.

THINK BIG **What do you like doing? Read and circle.**

using the computer writing reading

listening cutting gluing

watching a DVD playing a game

6 Look and match. Then say.

1 What's she doing?

She's listening to a story.

2 What are they doing?

They're watching a DVD.

3 What's he doing?

He's gluing shapes.

a

b

c

11 7 Listen. Follow the path.

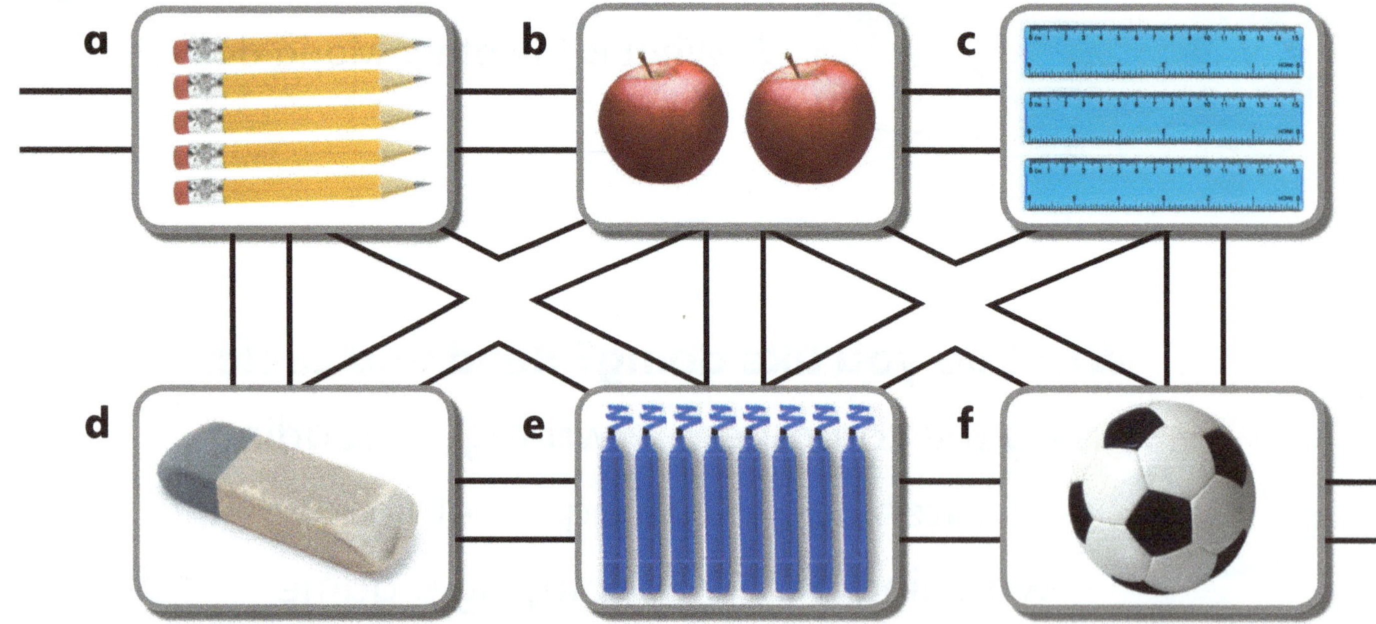

Language in Action

8 Look and write.

are they (x2) He's (x2) She's They're (x2) What's he (x2) What's she

1 What ________ doing? ________ listening.

2 ____________ doing? ________ cutting.

3 ____________ doing? ________ coloring.

4 What ________ doing? ________ playing a game.

5 ____________ doing? ________ counting.

9 Look at 8. Read and ✓.

1 There are ☐ one ball. ☐ four backpacks.

2 There's ☐ one ball. ☐ four backpacks.

10 Write the words and the number.

equals (x2) minus plus

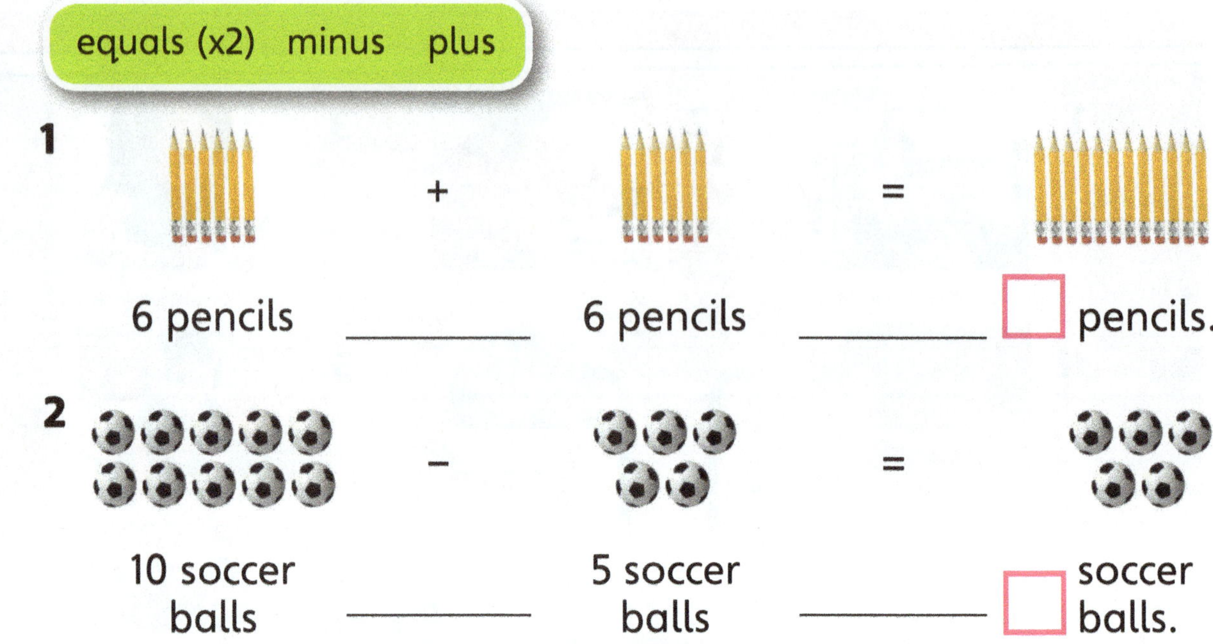

1 6 pencils ______ 6 pencils ______ ☐ pencils.

2 10 soccer balls ______ 5 soccer balls ______ ☐ soccer balls.

17 11 Listen and read. Write + or –, =, and the number.

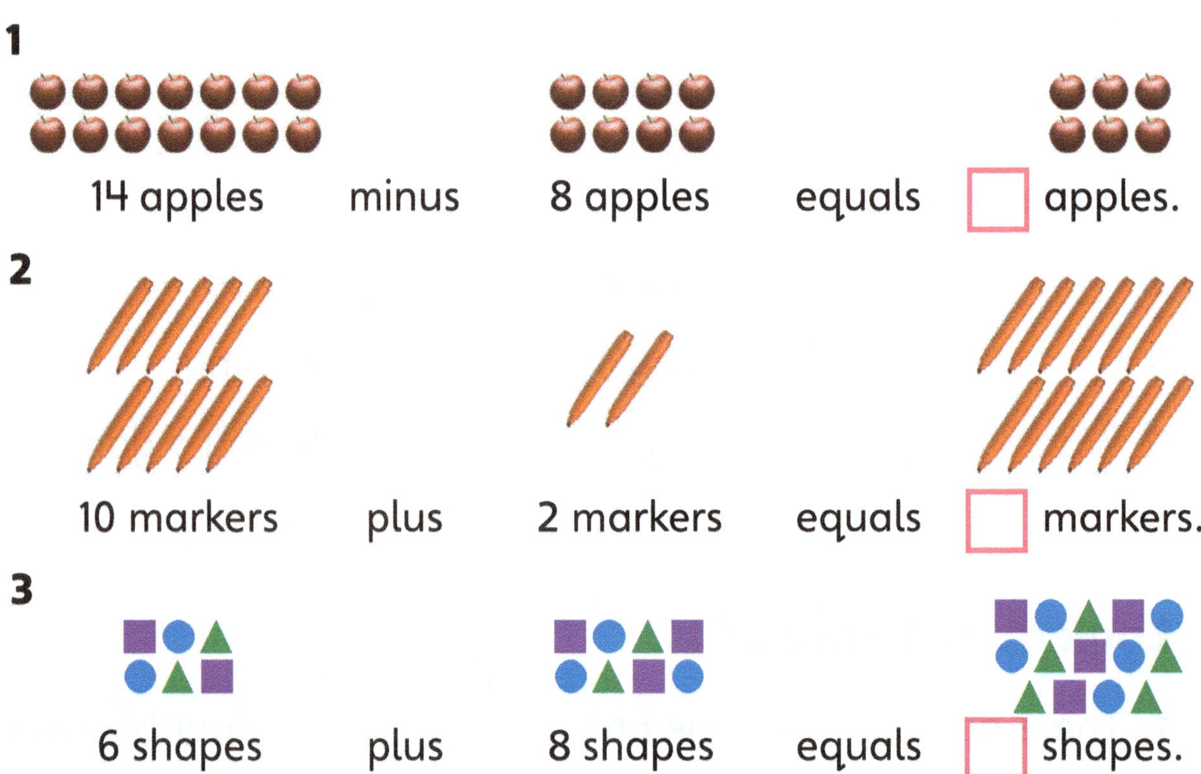

1 14 apples minus 8 apples equals ☐ apples.

2 10 markers plus 2 markers equals ☐ markers.

3 6 shapes plus 8 shapes equals ☐ shapes.

12 Look at 11. Match and write 1–3.

☐ **a** Six plus eight equals fourteen.
☐ **b** Fourteen minus eight equals six.
☐ **c** Ten plus two equals twelve.

13 Write the sums using numbers, +, –, and =. Then do the sums.

1 sixty plus seven equals ?

____

2 eighty-six minus three equals ?

____

3 twenty-three plus thirty-one equals ?

____

4 seventy-four minus twelve equals ?

____

5 sixty plus ten equals ?

____

6 thirty minus nineteen equals ?

____

THINK BIG **Write. What two things do you count every day in your classroom?**

________________ and ________________

14 Read and match.

1 Write.
2 Don't play a game.
3 Don't use the computer.
4 Count.

a

b

c

d

15 Read and circle.

1 **Stand** / **Sit** down.
2 Don't **stand** / **be** up!
3 **Write** / **Close** your books.
4 Don't **color** / **write** the picture.
5 **Open** / **Write** your name.
6 Don't **listen to** / **talk** in class.

16 Look and write.

cut ✗ eat ✗ listen ✓ write ✓

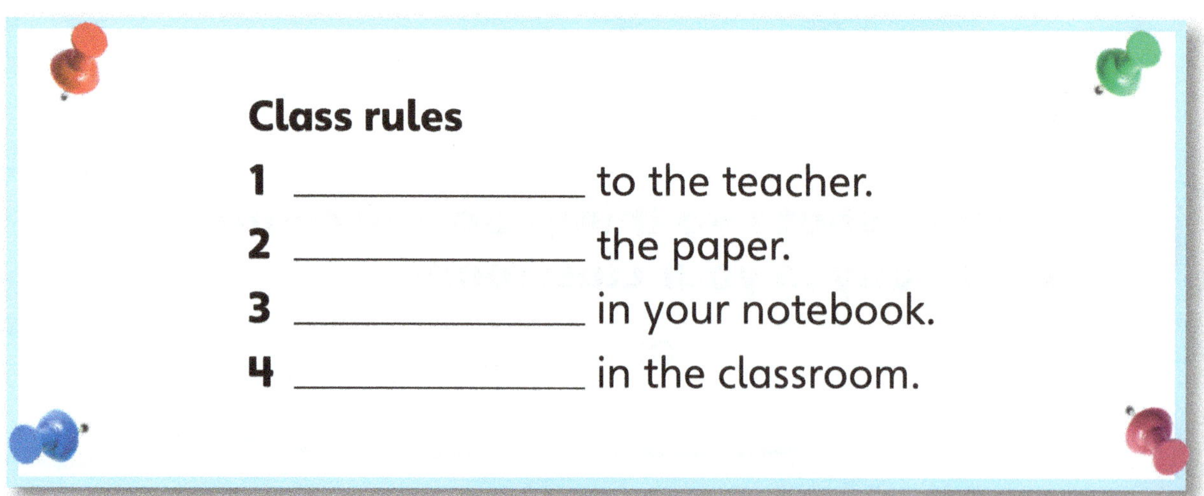

Class rules

1 ______________ to the teacher.
2 ______________ the paper.
3 ______________ in your notebook.
4 ______________ in the classroom.

17 Look at the pictures in 18. Read and write.

cold flowers open trees

1 It's ____________ in the mountains.
2 There are tall ____________ in the forest.
3 The school on the boat isn't closed. It's ____________.
4 There are colorful ____________ in the garden.

20 18 Listen, read, and match. Write a–d.

1 They're studying in a classroom on ☐

2 They're growing plants and flowers in ☐

3 They're having a P.E. class in ☐

4 They're studying animals in ☐

a a forest in Turkey. There are a lot of animals and birds in the trees.
b a boat in Bangladesh. This school is always open.
c a garden in the United States. It's a science class.
d the snow in France. The school is in the mountains.

19 Look at 18. Read and write.

Bangladesh France the United States Turkey

1 The students in ________________ are in the forest.
2 There is a garden at the school in ________________.
3 The boat school is in ________________.
4 The students in ________________ are in the mountains.

20 Find and write the sentences. Then match.

1 country. wet It a is

____

2 trees are There the in forest.

____

3 children skiing. The love

____

4 garden. are There flowers the in

____

a France

b the United States

c Turkey

d Bangladesh

Circle and draw.

THINK BIG

My favorite classroom is **in the mountains / in a forest / on a boat / in a garden.**

Values | Take turns.

21 Read and match. Then say.

1 May I use the markers now?

2 Yes, let's take turns!

3 It's fun taking turns!

a 

b 

c 

22 Read and write.

fun Let's May now

Anita: __________ I use the computer __________?
Sam: Yes! __________ take turns.
Anita: OK. It's __________ taking turns!

23 Find and circle the letters th.

24 Read and circle the letters th.

1 bath 2 path 3 this 4 that

25 Match the words with the same sounds.

1 they

2 math

a thin

b then

26 Listen and chant.

26

There are three
Crocodiles taking a bath.
They have thin mouths,
But big teeth!
Look out! Look out!

27 Look and write.

counting cutting playing a game using the computer

1 What's she doing?
She's ________________.

2 What's he doing?
He's ________________.

3 What are they doing?
They're ________________.

4 What are they doing?
They're ________________.

28 Count and write the numbers. Circle There's or There are.

<table>
<tr><th colspan="2">Our Classroom</th></tr>
<tr><td>computer</td><td>|</td></tr>
<tr><td>chairs</td><td>||||| ||||| |||||
|||</td></tr>
<tr><td>erasers</td><td>||||| |||</td></tr>
<tr><td>desks</td><td>||||| ||||</td></tr>
<tr><td>teacher</td><td>|</td></tr>
</table>

1 **There's / There are** ____ computer.

2 **There's / There are** ____ chairs.

3 **There's / There are** ____ erasers.

4 **There's / There are** ____ desks.

5 **There's / There are** ____ teacher.

29 Find the words. Circle.

coloring counting cutting gluing listening writing

e	s	g	l	u	i	n	g	m	c
m	i	n	g	i	l	u	r	e	o
n	g	a	t	f	a	s	g	k	u
g	o	t	a	l	k	i	n	g	n
c	o	l	o	r	i	n	g	u	t
u	n	g	t	u	n	g	l	d	i
t	g	o	i	f	g	a	u	g	n
t	l	i	s	t	e	n	i	n	g
i	s	w	r	i	t	i	n	g	a
n	p	a	e	n	t	t	g	i	t
g	i	f	o	i	a	s	f	n	o

30 Circle and write.

1 11 markers + / – ☐ markers = 7 markers

2 18 pencils + / – ☐ pencils = 20 pencils

3 13 books + / – ☐ books = 1 book

31 Complete the table.

Write your name.	1 ______________
Listen.	2 ______________
3 ______________	Don't open your book.
Sit here.	4 ______________
5 ______________	Don't use a pencil.

My Games

1 Read and match. Then say.

1 doing gymnastics

a

2 flying kites

b

c

3 ice-skating

4 skateboarding

d

e

5 playing tennis

f

6 climbing trees

33

2 Listen and sing. Then match.

a

b

Come On and Play

We're playing on the playground.
There are a lot of games to play.
Soccer, tennis, and volleyball.
What do you want to play today?

Paul likes playing on the swings.
Emma likes running and climbing.
We all love riding our bikes.
Tell us! What do you like doing?

c

d

We're playing on the playground.
It's always so much fun.
Come on and play with us.
We play with everyone!

3 Draw. Then say.

4 Read and write.

1 What does Jamie like doing?

He likes ______________________.

2 What does Jenny love doing?

She loves ______________________.

3 What does Tony love doing?

He loves ______________________.

4 What do they all like doing?

They like ______________________.

Circle the odd one out.

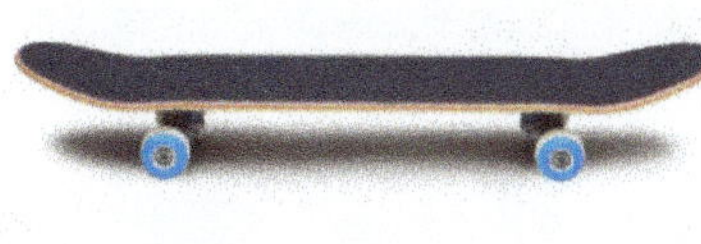

5 Write **do** or **does**. Then listen and match.

1 What ____________ he love doing?

2 What ____________ they like doing?

3 What ____________ she like doing?

4 What ____________ they love doing?

a

b

c

d

6 Look at 5. Write the answers.

1 He loves ________________________.

2 They like ________________________.

3 She likes ________________________.

4 They love ________________________.

7 Read and ✓.

1 I like skateboarding.

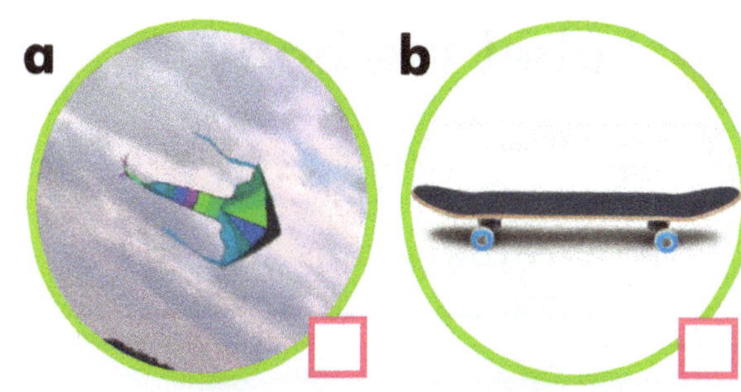

2 He loves playing tennis.

3 They like playing volleyball.

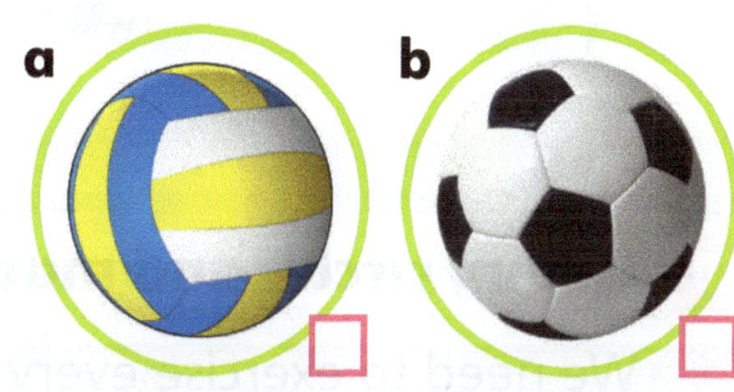

4 She likes climbing trees.

8 Look at 7. Write the questions.

1 ______________________________

2 ______________________________

3 ______________________________

4 ______________________________

9 Label the body.

bone finger foot
hand muscle

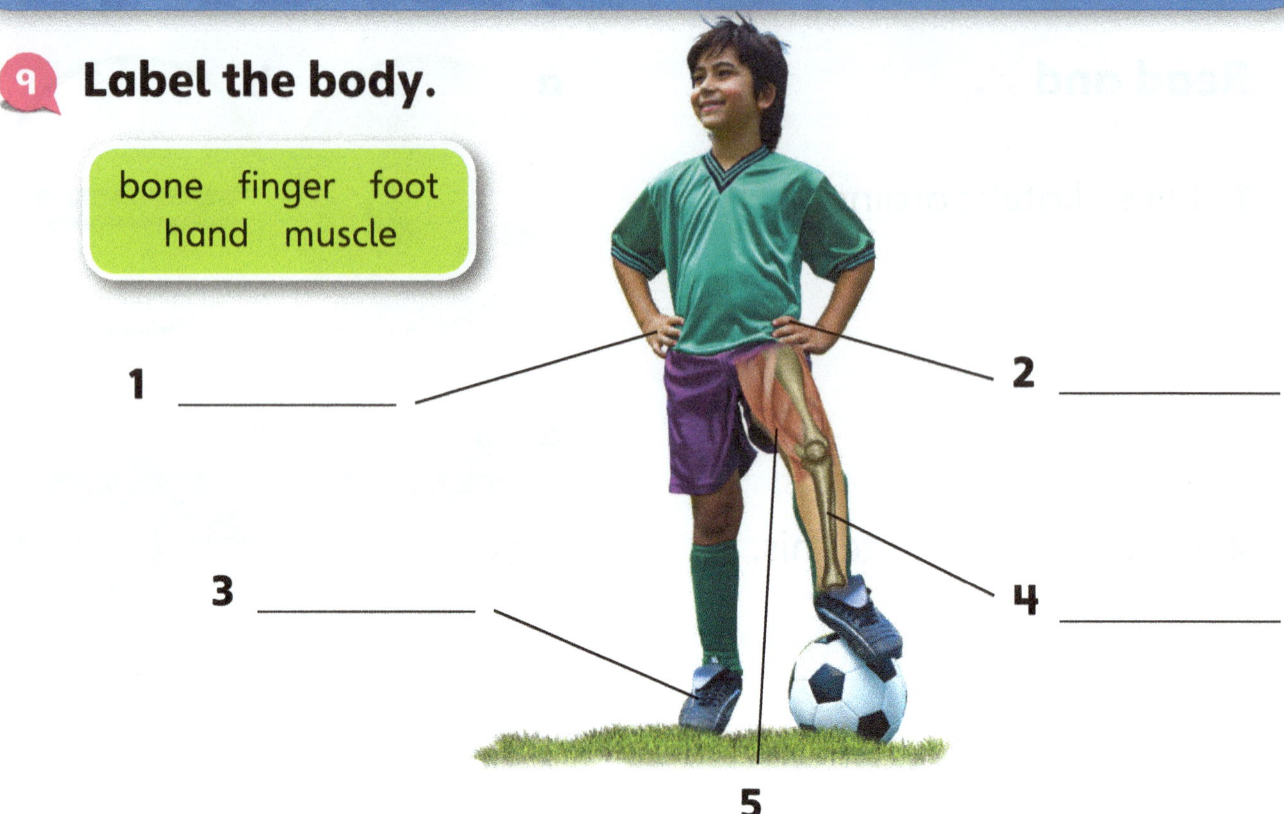

10 Listen, circle, and match.

We need to exercise every day. Exercise makes our **hands** / **muscles** strong. When we don't exercise, our bodies grow **big** / **weak**.

1 **Milk** / **Cake**, yogurt, and cheese help make our **bones** / **feet** strong, too.

2 There are **27** / **70** bones in one hand. When we throw a ball, we use **43** / **34** muscles.

3 There are **20** / **26** bones in one foot. When we kick a ball, we use **13** / **30** muscles.

4 When we jump, we use more than **17** / **70** muscles.

a 

b 

c 

d 

11 Look at 10. Circle T for true and F for false.

1 Milk makes our bodies weak. T F

2 There aren't many bones in our hands. T F

3 We use muscles to help us jump. T F

4 We use muscles in our feet when we throw a ball. T F

5 We don't need to exercise every day. T F

6 When we kick a ball, we use our feet. T F

12 Read and write.

Exercise kick move throw weak

1 __________ makes our muscles strong.

2 When we don't exercise, our muscles grow __________.

3 When I jump, I __________ my body.

4 I __________ a ball with my foot.

5 I __________ a ball with my hands.

THINK BIG

What parts of our body do we use when ice-skating? Check (✓).

bones ☐ legs ☐ nose ☐

arms ☐ mouth ☐ muscles ☐

13 Read and circle. Then match.

1 The children **doesn't / don't** like flying kites.

2 I **don't / doesn't** like climbing trees.

3 He **doesn't / don't** like playing tennis.

4 She **doesn't / don't** like doing gymnastics.

a b

c

d

14 Find and write the sentences.

1 love | dancing. | We

____

2 doesn't | basketball. | like | She | playing

____

3 don't | They | exercising. | like

____

4 I | skateboarding. | love

____

15 Read and write too or neither.

1 I love playing volleyball. — Me, __________.

2 Hulya doesn't like riding bikes. — Me __________.

3 We don't like skating. — Me __________.

4 My brother loves playing soccer. — Me, __________.

16 Look at the pictures in 17. Read and circle.

1 You play mancala with **stones** / **marbles**.

2 You **hit** / **catch** marbles with your finger.

3 You need a **ball** / **stone** to play jacks.

42 17 Listen, read, and match.

1 Mancala is a game from Ghana. It's for two people.

2 In Guatemala, children play this game on their own or with friends.

3 In India, a lot of people play this game together.

a You throw the ball, pick up the jacks, then catch the ball.

b You hit a marble with your finger. You win your friends' marbles.

c You move some stones around a board. You catch your friend's stones.

18 Look at 17. Write marbles, jacks, or mancala.

1 Two people play this game. ________

2 You can play this game on your own. ________

3 You play this game with a board. ________

4 You hit them with your finger. ________

5 You throw and catch a ball. ________

19 Read and write.

ball fingers Guatemala mancala marbles stones

1 In ______________, children like playing jacks. They use a ______________ and ten jacks.

2 In Ghana, children like playing ______________. They use a board and some ______________.

3 In India, children like playing ______________. They use their ______________.

THINK BIG

Circle. Which need a ball?

climbing playing jacks doing gymnastics
playing tennis playing volleyball riding a bike
running skateboarding swimming

20 Read and match.

1

a Always wear a helmet and knee pads.

2

b Always put one leg on each side.

3

c Always sit down on the swing.

4

d Always slide with your feet in front of you.

21 **Find and circle the letters ng and nk.**

22 **Read and circle the letters ng and nk.**

1 ring 2 pink 3 bang 4 ink

23 **Match the words with the same sounds.**

1 wing
2 bank

a sink
b sing

49

24 **Listen and chant.**

Sing a song about a king.
Thank you! Thank you!
He has a big, pink ring
And big, blue wings.
Thank you! Thank you!

25 Look and write.

1 What does she love doing? She loves ______________________.

2 What ______________________ he like doing? He likes

______________________.

3 What does he ______________________? He

______________________.

4 What does she love ______________________? She

______________________.

26 Read and write.

bones feet hands kick

1 We kick with our ________.
2 One hand has 27 ________.
3 When we ________ a ball, we use 13 muscles.
4 We throw with our ________.

27 Read and circle. Then ✓ or ✗ for you.

1 I like playing volleyball. **Me, too. / Me neither.** ☐
2 Elena doesn't like climbing trees. **Me, too. / Me neither.** ☐
3 My mom doesn't have a skateboard. **Me, too. / Me neither.** ☐
4 I love riding my bike. **Me, too. / Me neither.** ☐
5 I don't like doing gymnastics. **Me, too. / Me neither.** ☐

28 Draw and write.

In My House

1 Look and write the names of the rooms. Then match.

bathroom
bedroom
kitchen
living room

a b c d e f g h i

bed
chair
closet
couch
dresser
fridge
table
TV
shelf

2 Look at 1. What's in the rooms? Write.

1 There's a _______________, a _______________, and a _______________ in the bedroom.

2 There's a _______________, a _______________, and a _______________ in the living room.

3 There's a _______________, a _______________, and a _______________ in the kitchen.

55

3 Listen and sing. Circle the pictures from the song.

4 Look in your house. Count and write the number.

1 There are ____________ chairs in the living room.

2 There are ____________ chairs in the bedroom.

3 There are ____________ chairs in the kitchen.

4 There are ____________ chairs in the dining room.

5 Read and circle.

Where are your cousins now?

They're in the kitchen. Look!

1 The boys are Jamie's **brothers** / **cousins**.

2 The boys' mother is Jamie's **aunt** / **uncle**.

3 The boys are in the **bedroom** / **kitchen**.

4 The TV is in the **kitchen** / **living room**.

THINK BIG

Count and write the number.

How many cousins do you have? ☐

How many aunts do you have? ☐

How many uncles do you have? ☐

6 Read and match.

1 in front of   2 between   3 next to   4 behind

a   b    c    d

7 Follow, write, and circle.

chair (x2)   couch   kitchen

1 ____________ the table?
____________ **next to / behind**
the ____________.

2 ____________ my keys?
____________ **in front of /**
behind the ____________.

3 ____________ his shoes?
____________ **on / between**
the ____________.

4 ____________ the oven?
____________ **in / in front of**
the ____________.

a   b    c    d

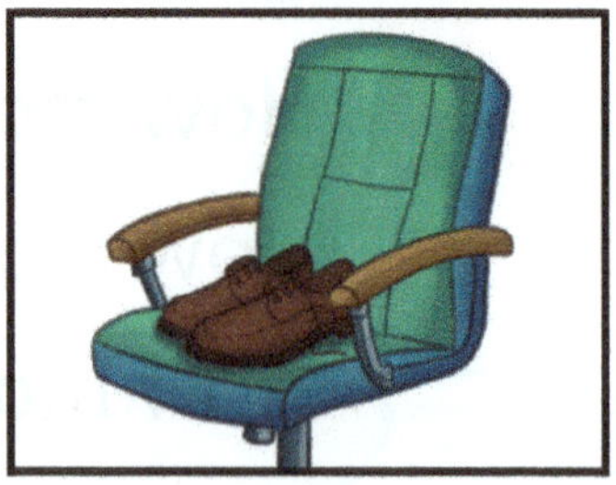

Language in Action

8 **Look and write. Use 's.**

1 Dan / 

They're ______________________.

2 Suzie / 

It's ______________________.

3 my mom / 

It's ______________________.

4 her brother / 

It's ______________________.

9 **Read the puzzles. Look at 8. Then write.**

1 It's behind the table, next to the chair. What is it?

____

2 It's on the table, between the lamp and the bike. What is it?

____

3 They're on the chair behind the kite. What are they?

____

4 It's on the dressing table, next to the backpack. What is it?

____

10 Write the names of the objects. Then write old or new.

bike computer fridge lamp phone TV

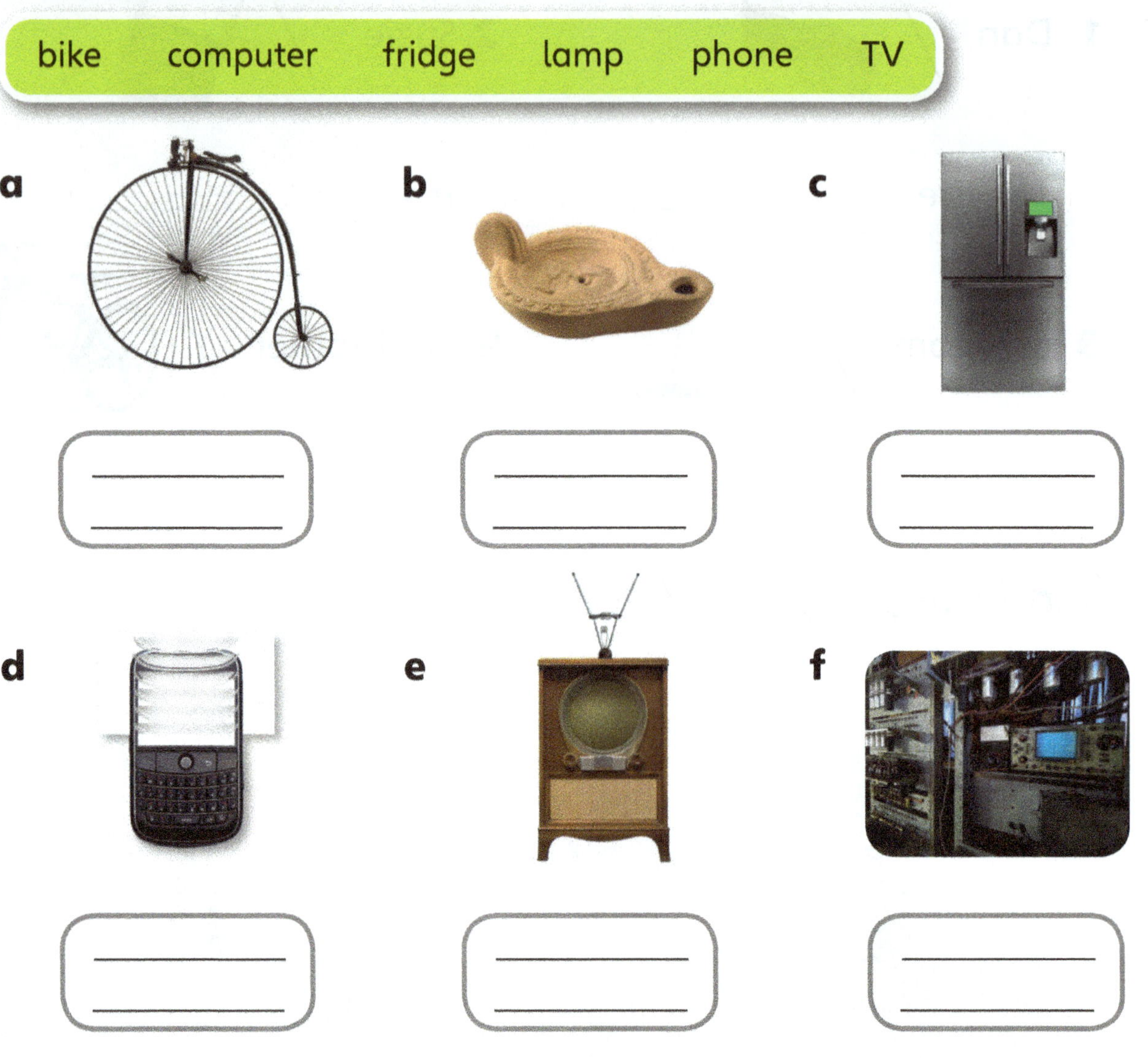

a
b
c
d
e
f

60 11 Listen and read. Match to the old objects in 10.

1 It's nearly 2,000 years old. It needs oil in it. The oil burns. ☐

2 Today we put them in our backpacks. But you can't put this one in your backpack. It needs a big room! ☐

3 It's very big and heavy, but the screen is very small. ☐

4 It has two wheels – a big wheel and a small wheel. When you ride it, you sit on the big wheel. It's fun! ☐

12 Look at 11. Read and match.

1 The old lamp needs

2 The oil in the lamp

3 The old computer

4 You can't put the old computer

5 The old TV has

6 The old bike

a a small screen.

b has a small wheel and a big wheel.

c oil.

d needs a big room.

e in a backpack.

f burns.

13 Look, read, and ✓.

1 This bathtub is new. ☐ This bathtub is old. ☐

2 This jacket is new. ☐ This jacket is old. ☐

3 This is a new phone. ☐ This is an old phone. ☐

4 These are new skates. ☐ These are old skates. ☐

THINK BIG **Draw one old thing and one new thing that are in your house.**

14 Read and match.

1 I have a dog. It's
2 You have a red pen. It's
3 My sister has a new coat. It's
4 My brother has a blue bike. It's
5 The children have a new ball. It's
6 My friends and I have some apples. They're

a ours.
b his.
c theirs.
d mine.
e hers.
f yours.

15 Complete the table.

I	mine
you	1 ___________
she	2 ___________
he	3 ___________
they	4 ___________
we	5 ___________

16 Read and write.

hers His Mine our Theirs yours

1 **Teacher:** Are those red pens ___________, Emma?
Emma: No, they aren't. ___________ are green.

2 **Teacher:** Do the boys have a pink ball?
Girls: No, they don't. ___________ is red and white. We have a pink ball. That's ___________ ball.

3 **Teacher:** Is this Lucy's blue coat?
Bella: No, it isn't ___________. It's Peter's. ___________ coat is blue, and Lucy's is purple.

17 Read and match.

1 You sit on a

2 You keep food cold in a

3 You sleep in a

4 You cook food in an

a bed.

b chair.

c oven.

d fridge.

63 18 Listen, write, and match.

Indonesia Japan Mali Sudan

1 These people are sitting in a restaurant in ___________.

2 This is a clay pot. But in ___________, people don't cook food in it.

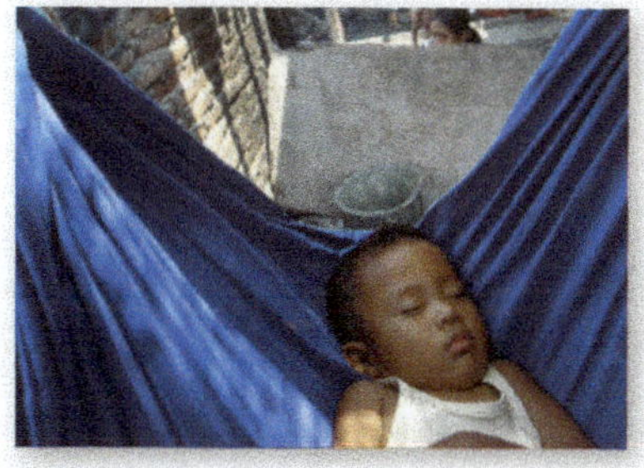

3 Some people in ___________ don't sleep in beds.

4 Some people in ___________ use a solar oven.

a They keep food cold in it, and it doesn't need electricity.

b It doesn't need fuel. It cooks food quickly in the sun.

c The chairs don't have legs, but they're very comfortable.

d They sleep in hammocks. When they don't need them, they put them in a closet.

19 Look at 18 and write.

closet pot restaurant sun

1 The chairs are in a Japanese ________.

2 The clay ________ doesn't need electricity.

3 Some people in Indonesia keep their hammocks in a ________.

4 A solar oven cooks food in the ________.

20 Read and ✓.

		a		b	
1	It needs electricity.	a fridge	☐	a clay pot in Sudan	☐
2	You keep it in a closet.	a bed	☐	a hammock	☐
3	It needs fuel.	a solar oven	☐	an oven	☐
4	It has legs.	my chair	☐	a Japanese chair	☐

THINK BIG

Circle and write about your home.

In my kitchen, there **is / are** ________ and ________.

In my living room, there **is / are** ________ and ________.

Values | Be neat.

21 **Listen and number. Then say.**

a

I put my dirty dishes in the sink.

b

I put my dirty clothes in the washing machine.

c

I put my toys in the toy box.

22 **Find and write the words.**

1 ______________________

2 ______________________

3 ______________________

xbo yot niks ngihsaw hcamein

23 **How do you keep your bedroom neat? Draw and write.**

I ____.

24 Find and circle the letters oo.

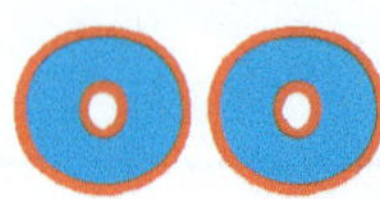

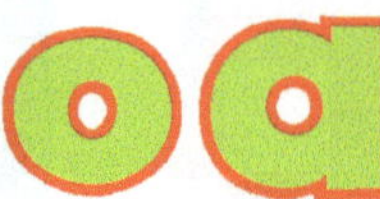

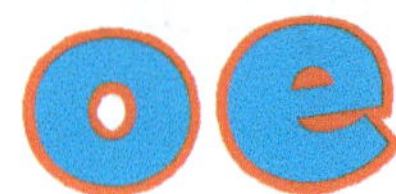

25 Read and circle the letters oo.

1 moon
2 book
3 zoo
4 foot

26 Match the words with the same sounds.

1 food
2 good

a look
b cool

70 27 Listen and chant.

Look in my
Cookbook.
The food is good!
The food is cool!

28 Look and write.

bathtub bed chair fridge lamp oven sink TV

29 Look at 28. Match.

1 Where's the oven?
2 Where's the bathtub?
3 Where are the chairs?

a They're in the dining room.
b It's in the kitchen next to the sink.
c It's in the bathroom.

30 Look at 28. Write.

1 What's in the bedroom?

There's a ____________, a ____________, a ____________, and a ____________.

2 What's in the living room?

There's a ____________, a ____________, a ____________, and a ____________.

31 Look and write. Where is Milo?

behind   between   in front of   next to

1 ______________

2 ______________

3 ______________

4 ______________

32 Look, read, and circle.

1 This computer is **old** / **new**.

2 These chairs are **new** / **old**.

3 This phone is **old** / **new**.

4 These are **old** / **new** cars.

33 Read and match.

1 That bike is Marta's.

2 Bella's mom and dad have a car.

3 Is this your toy?

4 It's Dan's skateboard.

5 These are our books.

a It's theirs.

b They're ours.

c It's hers.

d Yes, it's mine.

e It's his.

1 **Look, find, and number.**

2 **Look and find. Circle.**

At your school:
What do you like doing in the classroom? Circle one activity in red.

On the playground:
What do you like doing on the playground? Circle one activity in green.

In your house:
What do you have in your bedroom? Circle one thing in blue.

3 **Think, look, and draw.**

One thing is in the bedroom, in the classroom, and in the playground. What is it?

MY CLASSROOM

1 cutting
2 gluing
3 using the computer

MY GAMES

4 playing on the seesaw

5 playing on the slide

6 playing on the swing

MY HOUSE

7 a bed

8 a dresser

9 a lamp

unit 4 In My Town

1 Look and match.

1 shopping mall

2 train station

3 movie theater

4 bank

5 restaurant

6 supermarket

a

b

c

d

e

f

79

2 Listen and sing. Circle the places on the map.

Maps Are Great!

Where's the bookstore?
I want to buy a book.
Here, I have a map.
Come on. Let's take a look!

The bookstore is on River Street.
It isn't far from us.
Do you want to walk there?
No, thanks! Let's take the bus!

I want to send a letter, too.
Is there a post office, do you know?

I'm looking at the map. Yes, there is.
It's near the bookstore. Come on. Let's go.

Maps are really great.
I use them every day.
In town or out of town,
They help me find my way!

3 What's in your town? Check (✓).

- ☐ bookstore
- ☐ post office
- ☐ bus stop
- ☐ gas station
- ☐ computer store

4 Read and ✓.

Is There a Bookstore?

What's in the shopping mall?

- ☐ There's a bookstore.
- ☐ There's a movie theater.
- ☐ There's a computer store.
- ☐ There are restaurants.
- ☐ There are supermarkets.

What is there in your town? Read and circle.

bank   bus stop   computer store
gas station   shopping mall
train station

5 Look and write want to or wants to.

1 I ____________ eat pizza.

2 Amy ____________ go to the supermarket.

3 Lisa ____________ buy a computer.

4 My brother ____________ send a letter.

6 Write.

I want to go ____________
____________.
I ____________
____
____________.

Mom wants to ____________
____________.
She ____________
____
____________.

7 Draw a post office and a bookstore.

8 Look at 7. Write Yes, there is or No, there isn't.

1 Is there a bus stop on Pine Street?

____

2 Is there a train station on Pine Street?

____

3 Is there a supermarket next to the post office?

____

4 Is there a movie theater between the post office and the bookstore?

____

5 Is there a gas station near the bus stop?

____

6 Is there a restaurant next to the movie theater?

____

9 Look, read, and write.

bike boat bus train

1 In London, some children go to school by  ________.

2 In Mexico City, many children go to school by  ________.

3 In Bangkok, many children go to school by  ________.

4 In Beijing, many children go to school by  ________.

10 Listen, read, and write.

84

bike canals fast ground without

There are a lot of [1] ________ in Bangkok. Sunan goes to school by boat.

Lars and his friends live in Amsterdam. They go to school by [2] ________, on bike streets. Bike streets are safe streets [3] ________ cars.

In Mexico City, there a lot of cars on the street. Carmen goes to school by bus because it's [4] ________. Her school is near a bus stop.

Sophia goes to school under the [5] ________. There are 468 subway stations in New York! Sophia's apartment is near a station.

11 Look at 10. Circle T for true and F for false.

1 Sunan goes to school by car. T F

2 Cars don't go on bike streets in Amsterdam. T F

3 Carmen's school isn't near a bus stop. T F

4 Sophia lives near a subway station. T F

5 There are four hundred eighty-six subway stations in New York. T F

12 Read and write.

Amsterdam Bangkok Mexico City New York

1 There are a lot of cars on the streets. ____________

2 There are a lot of canals. ____________

3 There are safe bike streets. ____________

4 There are a lot of subway stations. ____________

THINK BIG

How do teachers go to school in your country? Check (✓).

boat ☐ train ☐ bus ☐

bike ☐ car ☐

13 Read and circle.

1 How much **is** / **are** those sandwiches?

2 How much **is** / **are** that banana?

3 How much **is** / **are** that bike?

4 How much **is** / **are** that pizza?

5 How much **is** / **are** those books?

6 How much **is** / **are** the toys?

14 Write the numbers.

1 five dollars and twenty-five cents $ ________

2 two dollars and ninety-nine cents $ ________

3 sixty-eight cents ________ ¢

4 ten dollars $ ________

5 one dollar and seventy-two cents $ ________

87 15 Listen and match.

1 $4.80   2 $1.75   3 $7.50   4 $19.99

a b c d

16 Read and write.

big modern new slow

1 It isn't old. It's ____________.

2 It isn't fast. It's ____________.

3 It isn't small. It's ____________.

4 It isn't from a long time ago. It's ____________.

89 17 Listen and read. Then circle and match.

1 In Havana, some taxis are **old** / **new**. New taxis are black and yellow.

2 In London, taxis have a **colorful** / **famous** design.

3 In Berlin, most taxis look the **same** / **cheap**.

4 Tuk tuks in New Delhi have three wheels. They're **cheap** / **fast**.

a They're green and yellow, and they're easy to find.

b They're light brown, and they're comfortable.

c They have three wheels, and they're fun to ride in.

d They look like cars from a long time ago. They're big and black.

18 **Look at 17 and match. Taxi words can be matched to more than one city.**

new	Havana	green and yellow
three wheels		look the same
black and yellow	New Delhi	comfortable
fun	Berlin	light brown
big and black		easy to find
cheap	London	famous design

THINK BIG

Draw a taxi in your city. Write about it.

My city is called

_______________.

Taxis in my city are

_______________ and

_______________.

Most of them are

_______________________.

They're

_______________________.

Values | Cross the street safely.

19 Read, look, and circle.

1 I **look** / **don't look** left, then right, then left again before I cross the street.

2 I wait for the **blue** / **green** man.

3 I **always** / **never** cross at the pedestrian crossing.

a

b

c

20 Find and write the words.

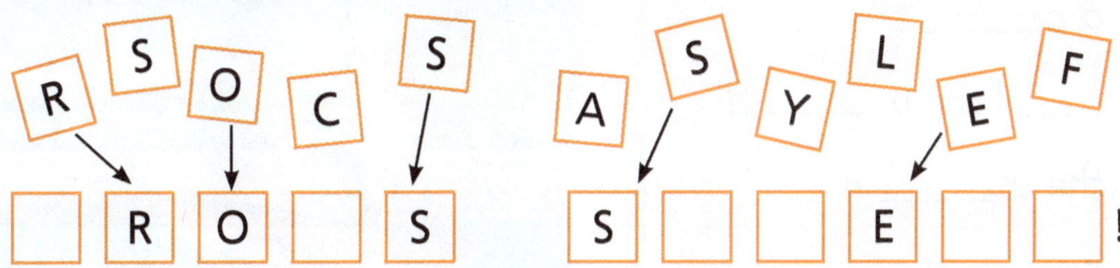

21 **Find and circle the letters ai and oa.**

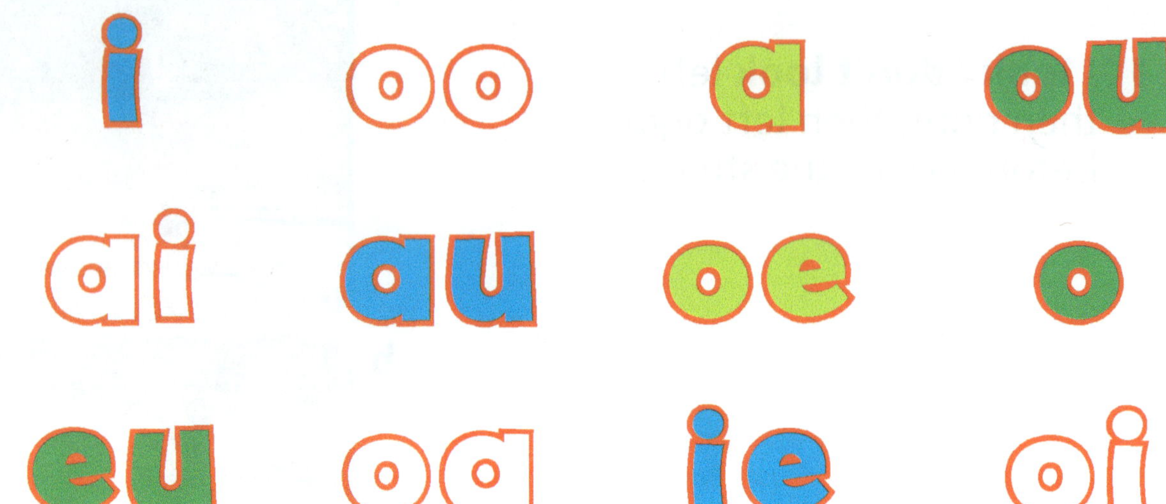

22 **Read and circle the letters ai and oa.**

23 **Match the words with the same sounds.**

1 road **a** wait

2 tail **b** soap

95

24 **Listen and write the letters. Then chant.**

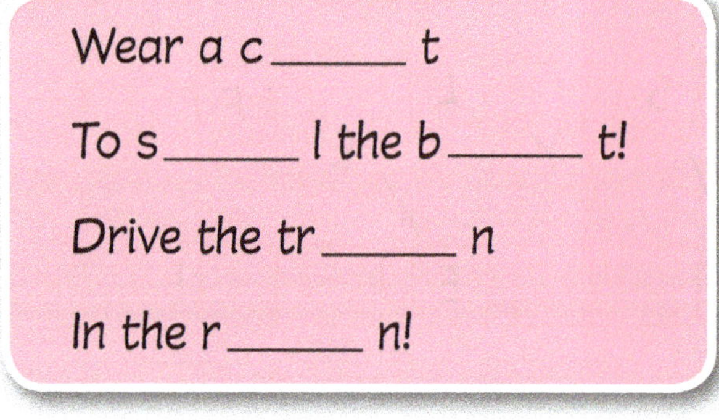

96 25 Listen and follow the path.

26 Look at 25. Write.

Where do they go?

1 ____________________ 2 ____________________

3 ____________________ 4 ____________________

5 ____________________

27 Write **want to** or **wants to**. Then match.

1 We ________ buy fruit.

2 She ________ go by train.

3 You ________ go to the bank.

4 He ________ buy gas.

a There's a bank on Elm Street.

b Is there a gas station near here?

c There's a supermarket behind the shopping mall.

d Is there a train station on London Road?

28 Look, read, and circle.

1 In Mexico City, many children go to school by **bus** / **boat**.

2 In China, many children go to school by **train** / **bike**.

3 In London, many children go to school by **boat** / **train**.

4 In Bangkok, many children go to school by **boat** / **bike**.

29 Read and circle.

1 How much **is** / **are** those games? — **They're** / **It's** $7.

2 How much **is** / **are** that skateboard? — **They're** / **It's** $17.99.

3 How much **is** / **are** those apples? — **They're** / **It's** 85¢.

4 How much **is** / **are** that hat? — **They're** / **It's** $4.85.

My Dream Job

1 Circle and match.

a	p	e	o	c	k	a
d	s	i	n	g	e	r
o	p	b	l	d	w	t
c	i	v	r	o	t	i
t	s	i	e	d	t	s
o	v	p	r	t	s	t
r	h	a	c	t	o	r

pilot

artist

singer

vet

doctor

actor

2 Look and circle.

1 chef / writer

2 athlete / dancer

102

3 Listen and chant. Then write.

pilot

actor

Hey, What Do You Want to Be?

Hey, what do you want to be?
You have to choose just one.
There are so many different jobs.
I want one that is fun!

I want to be a [1]__________
And an athlete, too.
Or maybe a [2]__________.
What about you?

I want to be an [3]__________,
And I want to be a vet.
I want to be a [4]__________, too.
Then I can fly a jet!

Chorus

teacher

dancer

4 Write and draw.

I want to be **a** / **an**
__________________.

5 Read and circle.

1 Jenny wants to be a **singer** / **writer**.

2 Dan wants to be a **writer** / **singer**.

3 Jenny and Dan are talking to their **friend** / **teacher**.

6 Read the story again. What do they like doing? Match.

1 eating

2 dancing

3 singing

4 writing

a 

b 

c 

d 

Read and circle. I like music. I want to be a _____________ and a _____________.

chef dancer singer writer

7 Look and write.

drawing flying singing writing

1

What do you want to be?

I ______ to be a singer. I like __________.

2

What do you want to be?

____________ an artist. I like __________.

3

What do you want to be?

__________________ a pilot. I __________.

4

What do you want to be?

____

____

8 What do you like doing? Write and draw.

I like ____________

________________.

9 Look and write.

1

______________________________?

She wants to be a dancer.

2

______________________________?

He wants to be a teacher.

3

______________________________?

She wants to be a doctor.

4

______________________________?

He wants to be an athlete.

10 Look and match. Then write.

cooking running

1 What does he want to be?

2 What does she want to be?

a She wants to be a chef. She likes ____________.

b He wants to be an athlete. He likes ____________.

11 Write. What do you want to be? Why?

____

____

____

12 Look and write.

farmer hairdresser waiter

1 ______________ 2 ______________ 3 ______________

107 13 Read and write. Then listen and check.

cut entertain grows makes sells takes

Goods are products. People produce goods: a farmer [1] ______________ food, and a carpenter [2] ______________ a table. People also buy and sell goods. Food, books, clothes, and houses are goods. Electronic books that you can read on a tablet are virtual goods.

Some people don't produce goods. They provide services. Hairdressers [3] ______________ your hair. Singers and actors [4] ______________ you. These are services.

A restaurant provides goods and services. It [5] ______________ goods (food and drink). It also provides a service when the waiter [6] ______________ the food to the tables.

14 Look at 13 and circle.

1 Goods are **services** / **products**.

2 When a carpenter makes a table, he's **providing a service** / **producing goods**.

3 An electronic book is a **product** / **service**.

4 When singers entertain you, they are **providing a service** / **selling a product**.

5 Restaurants provide **services** / **goods** / **services and goods**.

6 A waiter **sells products** / **provides a service**.

15 Write Goods or Services.

1 ____________

2 ____________

3 ____________

4 ____________

Read, guess, and write.

chef nurse pilot

I take care of sick people. Who am I? ____________

I fly a plane. Who am I? ____________

I cook food in a restaurant. Who am I? ____________

16 Read and match.

1 I want to be a singer
2 I'm at the post office
3 I want to be an artist
4 I'm at the hairdresser's
5 I want to buy this T-shirt

because

a it looks nice.
b I like painting pictures.
c I like entertaining people.
d I want to mail a letter.
e I need a new hairstyle.

17 Read and circle.

1 Let's go for a ride in that boat. It looks **tired** / **fun**.
2 Go to bed. You look **nice** / **tired**.
3 I want to read this book because it looks **good** / **kind**.
4 It looks **sunny** / **funny** outside. Let's go to the park.
5 Your new hairstyle looks **sick** / **nice**.
6 Go to the doctor. You look **happy** / **sick**.

18 Read and write. Use look or looks.

cold hot kind sick

1 I don't want to swim in the ocean. It ____________________.
2 Are you OK? You ____________________.
3 I think that woman is a teacher. She ____________________.
4 Be careful! That oil ____________________.

19 Match.

1 scuba

2 park

3 rodeo

a ranger

b rider

c diver

110 20 Listen and read. Match, then write the jobs in 19.

1 Katie wants to be a vet someday. She lives with her family in Oklahoma, in the United States.

☐ ____________________

2 Juma lives in Botswana, Africa. Many animals are in danger there.

☐ ____________________

3 José Antonio lives in Costa Rica near the ocean. His mom is a photographer.

☐ ____________________

a She loves the animals. She wants to help protect them someday. That's her father's job.

b He loves swimming. Sometimes he takes pictures of the colorful fish under the water.

c They have a lot of cows and horses because they live on a ranch. She loves riding horses.

21 Look at 20. Circle T for true and F for false.

1 Katie doesn't like horses. T F

2 The animals on the ranch are in danger. T F

3 Juma's father is a park ranger. T F

4 Juma doesn't want to work with animals someday. T F

5 José Antonio loves taking pictures of fish. T F

6 José Antonio's mother is a scuba diver. T F

22 Read and write.

Botswana colorful fish horses and cows
in danger the United States underwater camera

1 There are a lot of ____________________ in the ocean.

2 Some wild animals in Africa are ____________________.

3 There are ____________________ on a ranch.

4 Juma's home is in ____________________.

5 José Antonio uses his mom's ____________________.

6 Oklahoma is in ____________________.

THINK BIG

Which jobs would you like to try?
Put a ✓ or a ✗.

pilot ☐ doctor ☐ teacher ☐ scuba diver ☐
nurse ☐ vet ☐ writer ☐ rodeo rider ☐
mechanic ☐ park ranger ☐
hairdresser ☐ farmer ☐

23 Look, write, and match.

1 I like art.

2 I like science.

3 I like math.

4 I like music.

a 

I want to be a ____________.

b 

I want to be an ____________.

c 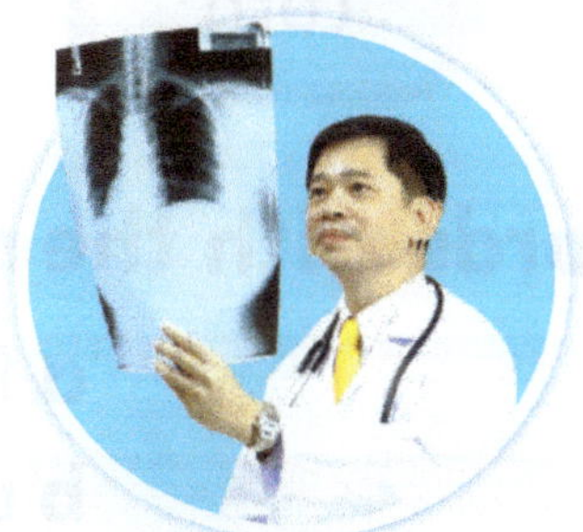

I want to be a ____________.

d 

I want to be a ____________.

24 Find and write the sentences.

1 math. I like ____________

2 I be to a want teacher. ____________

3 I art. like ____________

4 writer. want a to be I ____________

25 Find and circle the letters ar, er, and or.

26 Read and circle the letters ar, er, and or.

27 Match the words with the same sounds.

1 singer
2 born
3 cart

a for
b art
c letter

116

28 Listen and write the letters. Then chant.

29 Look and write. What do they want to be?

actor	artist	dancer	doctor
pilot	singer	teacher	vet

30 Look and write.

1 What does she want to be?

____

2 What does he want to be?

____

3 What does she want to be?

____

4 What does he want to be?

____

31 Complete the sentences with your own ideas. Use **because**.

1 I want to be a writer ______________________

______________________.

2 I want to be a park ranger ______________________

______________________.

unit 6 My Day

1 Listen and ✓. Then write.

1 a  ☐ b  ☐

2 a  ☐ b  ☐

3 a  ☐ b  ☐

4 a 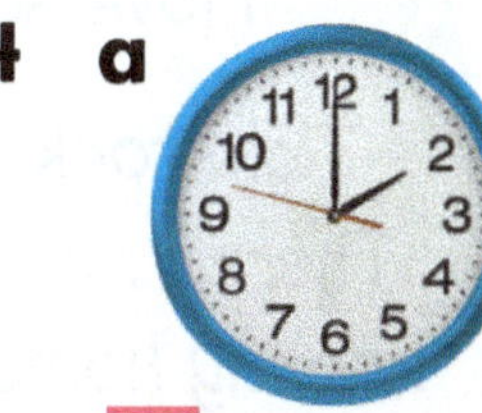 ☐ b  ☐

2 Read, draw, and say.

1

one o'clock

2

ten o'clock

123

3 Listen and sing. Look at the pictures. Then number in order.

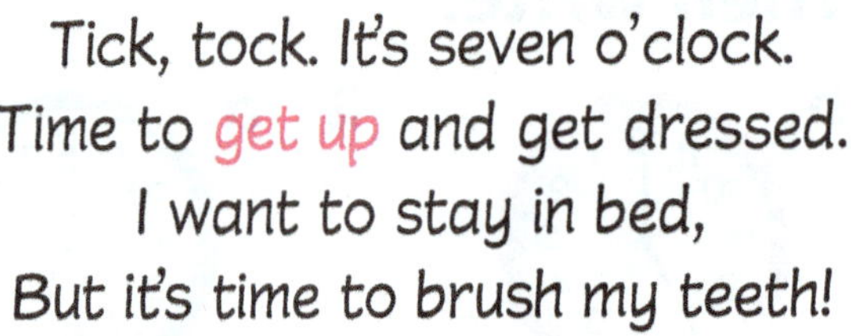

What Time Is It?

a

b

Tick, tock. It's seven o'clock.
Time to get up and get dressed.
I want to stay in bed,
But it's time to brush my teeth!

Tick, tock. It's eight o'clock.
At nine o'clock, I start school.
I eat my breakfast and get my books.
I love school, it's cool!

c

Tick, tock. It's three o'clock.
There's no more school today.
I do my homework, and I go out.
And there's my friend to play.

d

Now it's evening, and it's eight o'clock,
And it's time to go to bed.
I watch TV and read my book.
Time to sleep now, good night!

4 Look at 3. Write.

1 I get up at ______________________.

2 I start school at ______________________.

3 I go out at ______________________.

4 I go to bed at ______________________.

5 Read. Then write in order.

1 ____________________

2 ____________________

3 ____________________

4 ____________________

5 ____________________

- Max comes home.
- Max eats.
- Max gets up.
- Max goes out.
- Max sleeps again.

THINK BIG

How many hours do I sleep?

I go to bed at __________ in the evening.
I get up at __________ in the morning.
I sleep for __________ hours.

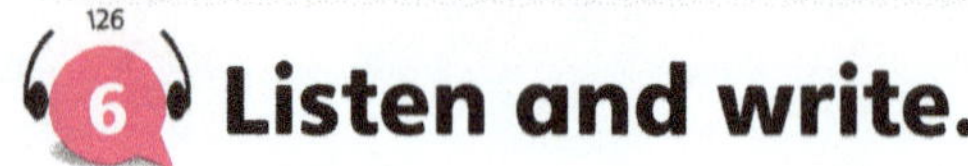

6 Listen and write.

1 get up: ____

2 start school: ____

3 finish school: ____

4 go out: ____

5 watch TV: ____

6 go to bed: ____

7 Look at 6. Write.

1 When do you get up?

2 When ____ you start school?

3 When ________ finish school?

4 ____________________ go out?

5 ________________________ TV?

6 ____________________________

1 I get up at ____________________.

2 I ____________ at ____________.

3 I ____________ at ____________.

4 ____________ at ____________.

5 ______________________________

6 ______________________________

8 **Read and circle. Then draw and write the time.**

1 When **do / does** she go out?
She **go out / goes out** at 4:00.

____

2 When **do / does** he watch TV?
He **watch / watches** TV at 5:00.

____

3 When **do / does** you go to bed?
I **go to bed / goes to bed** at 8:00.

____

4 When **do / does** they get up?
They **get up / gets up** at 7:00.

____

5 When **do / does** this movie start?
It **start / starts** at 10:00.

____

6 When **do / does** this movie finish?
It **finish / finishes** at 12:00.

____

9 Are these ways to tell the time new or old? Write new or old.

1 candle clock ____________ 2 clock ____________

3 hourglass ____________ 4 phone ____________

5 sundial ____________ 6 water clock ____________

7 watch ____________

10 Read and write. Then listen and check.

129

candle cups height hourglass sand shadow sundial water

This is a [1] ____________ clock. When it burns, it gets shorter. The [2] ____________ of the candle tells you the time. You can use this clock in the day and the night.

An [3] ____________ uses sand to tell the time. The [4] ____________ falls from the top to the bottom.

A [5] ____________ clock uses water to tell the time. It works like an hourglass. It has two [6] ____________. The water falls from one cup to the other.

A [7] ____________ uses the sun to tell the time. The sun makes a shadow on the sundial. The [8] ____________ tells the time.

11 Look at 10 and match.

1 A candle tells the time when it
2 The candle clock works in
3 The sundial needs
4 An hourglass uses
5 A water clock uses

a sand.
b water.
c burns.
d the day and the night.
e the sun.

12 Look at 10. Circle T for true and F for false.

1	A water clock doesn't work at night.	T	F
2	An hourglass uses a candle to tell the time.	T	F
3	The shadow tells you the time on a sundial.	T	F
4	A candle clock doesn't work in the sun.	T	F
5	A water clock has two glasses for the water.	T	F

13 Read and match.

1 Where
2 Who
3 What
4 When
5 How
6 How many

a is your favorite game?
b do you get up?
c children are there in your class?
d does your teacher get to school?
e are your best friends?
f do you live?

Twenty-five.
It's basketball!
Near the school.
At seven o'clock.
Eva and Rob.
By bus.

14 Find and write the sentences

1 your | work? | does | Where | dad

____

2 start? | the | When | party | does

____

3 spell | you | How | name? | do | your

____

15 Look and write. Use do, does, is, or are.

1 What __________ you like to do in your free time?
2 Who __________ your English teacher?
3 When __________ the movie finish?
4 How many chairs __________ in your classroom?
5 Where __________ your grandparents live?
6 How __________ an hourglass work?

16 Read and complete.

go have play start watch

1 We ____________ breakfast at 7 o'clock.

2 We ____________ school at 8 o'clock.

3 We ____________ home after school.

4 I ____________ TV at 6 o'clock.

5 I ____________ games with my friends.

132

17 Listen, read, and write.

5 o'clock 8 o'clock 9 o'clock 10 o'clock 12 o'clock two Sunday

Bruno lives in Brazil. He goes to school from 7 o'clock to [1] ____________. In the afternoon, he goes to a dance class. He has dinner at [2] ____________.

Jun lives in China. Her school starts at 8 o'clock and finishes at [3] ____________. They have a break for [4] ____________ hours at lunchtime. After dinner, Jun does homework, then she watches TV.

Ali lives in Egypt. He goes to school from [5] ____________ through Thursday because Friday is a holiday. Classes start at 8 o'clock. At [6] ____________ they have a break, and school finishes at 3 o'clock. After school, Ali plays with his sisters, then goes to bed at [7] ____________.

18 Look at 17 and circle.

1 Bruno goes to school for **4** / **5** hours.

2 He goes to a dance class **at** / **after** school.

3 Jun has a break at **lunchtime** / **dinnertime**.

4 Jun watches TV **after** / **before** dinner.

5 Ali doesn't go to school on **Thursday** / **Friday**.

6 Ali **plays** / **goes to bed** at 9 o'clock.

19 Read and write Bruno, Jun, or Ali.

1 ____________ likes to dance.

2 ____________ and ____________ start school at 8 o'clock.

3 ____________ finishes school at 12 o'clock

4 ____________ has dinner at 8 o'clock.

5 ____________ finishes school at 5 o'clock.

6 ____________ likes watching TV.

Write the times for you.

I get up at ____________.

I go to school from ____________ to ____________.

I have a break at ____________.

I have lunch at ____________.

I have dinner at ____________.

I go to bed at ____________.

20 School starts at 8:00. Help Anna get to school on time. Follow the paths and choose 🙂 or 🙁.

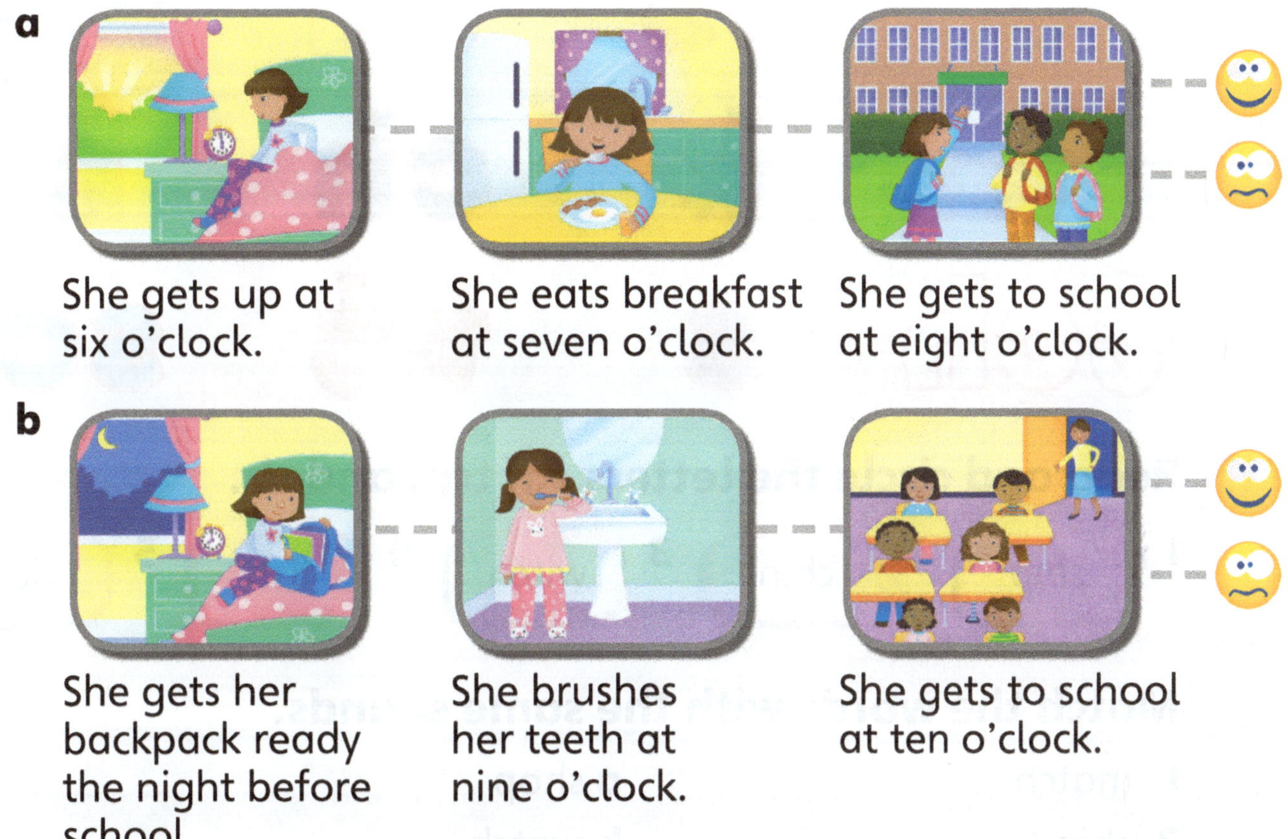

a

She gets up at six o'clock.

She eats breakfast at seven o'clock.

She gets to school at eight o'clock.

b

She gets her backpack ready the night before school.

She brushes her teeth at nine o'clock.

She gets to school at ten o'clock.

21 How do you get to school on time? Check (✓) and draw one step.

- ☐ I get up early on school days.
- ☐ I get dressed quickly and eat breakfast.
- ☐ I get my backpack ready the night before school.
- ☐ I always get to school on time.

22 Find and circle the letters ch, tch, and sh.

23 Read and circle the letters ch, tch, and sh.

1 ship 2 chin 3 witch 4 fish 5 rich

24 Match the words with the same sounds.

1 match	**a** shop
2 chip	**b** watch
3 dish	**c** lunch

138

25 Listen and write the letters. Then chant.

Watch the wi____,
She's having lun____!
Fries and fi____
From a di____!

26 Write the words. Then color the times.

brushes – green	finishes – brown	o'clock – orange
school – blue	six – purple	snack – red

1 I start ______________ at nine o'clock.

2 He ______________ his teeth at eight o'clock.

3 The movie ______________ at five o'clock.

4 They eat a ______________ at four o'clock.

5 She reads a book at seven ______________.

6 I eat chicken and salad at ______________ o'clock.

27 Look and write.

1 When ____________ they go out?

They ________________ at ____________.

2 When ____________ she get up?

She ________________ at ____________.

3 When ____________ he start school?

He ________________ at ____________.

28 Write about you. Add the times.

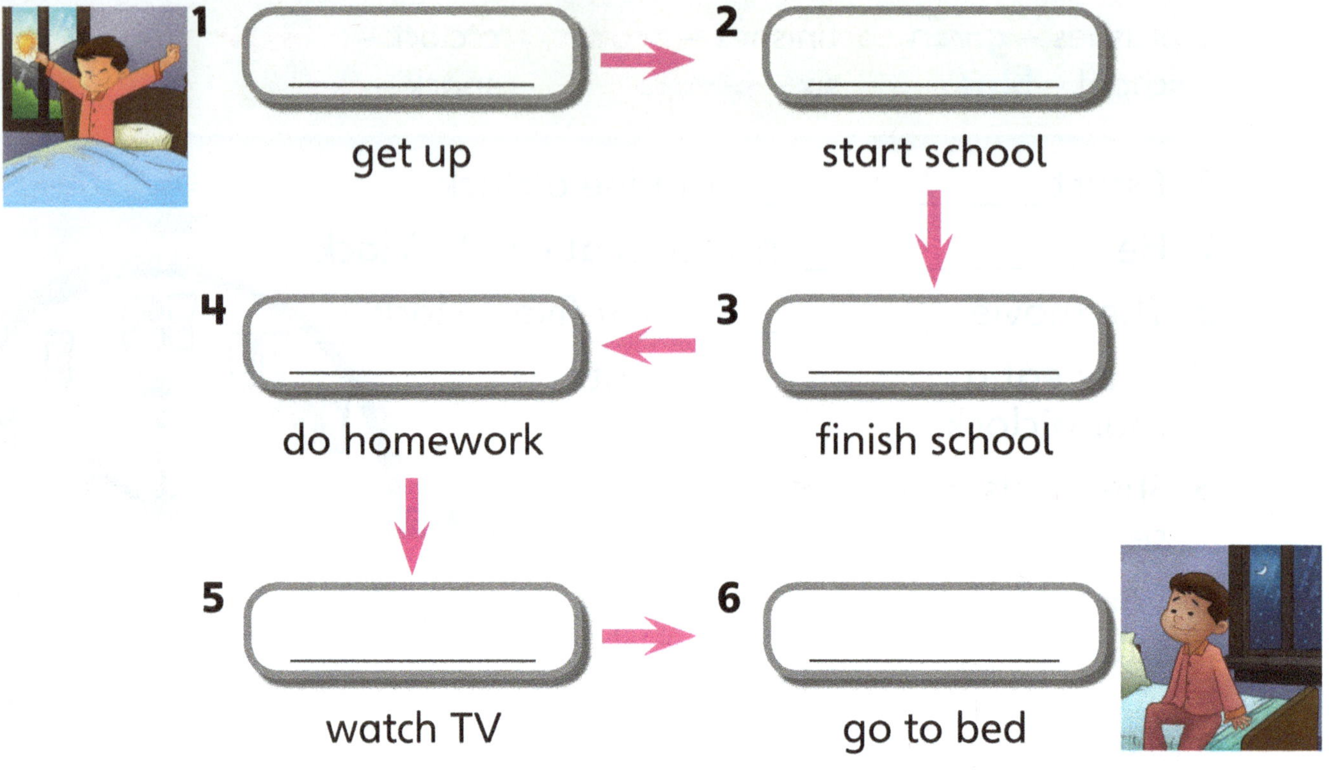

29 Circle. Then write answers for you.

1 **How** / **When** do you have breakfast?

____

2 **What** / **Who** is your favorite color?

____

3 What time **do** / **does** school finish?

____

4 **How** / **What** do you do after school?

____

5 How many books **do** / **does** you have in your bag today?

____

6 What **does** / **is** your teacher's name?

____

1 Look, find, and number.

2 Mark is visiting a small town. What can he do? Look at the town and ✓.

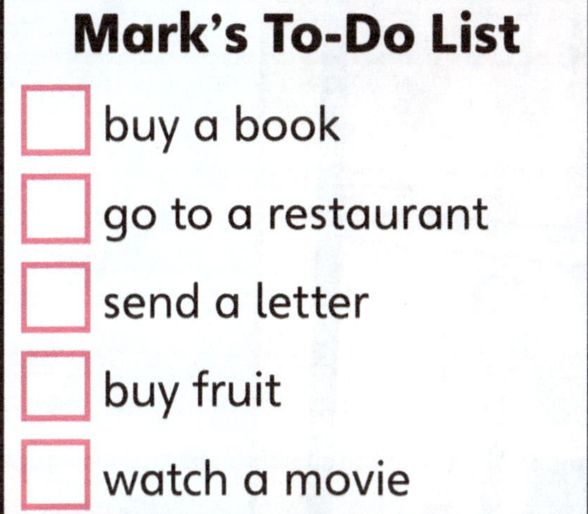

Mark's To-Do List

- [ ] buy a book
- [ ] go to a restaurant
- [ ] send a letter
- [ ] buy fruit
- [ ] watch a movie

3 Think and draw. In the town, there isn't a ______________.

MY TOWN

1 bus stop
2 computer store
3 supermarket

DREAM JOBS

4 artist
5 doctor
6 athlete

MY DAY

7 brush teeth
8 get up
9 go to bed

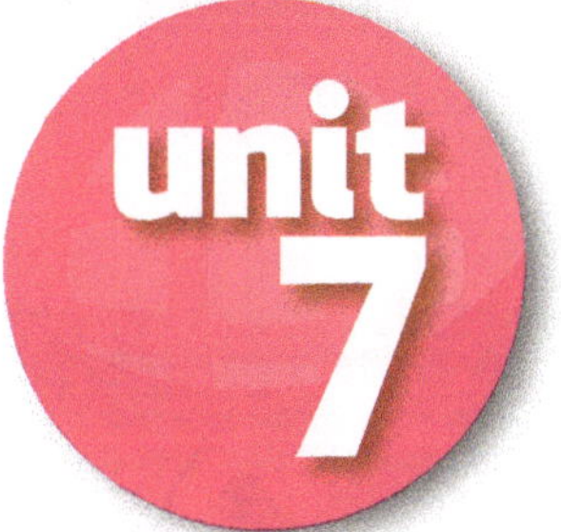

unit 7 My Favorite Food

1 Look and match.

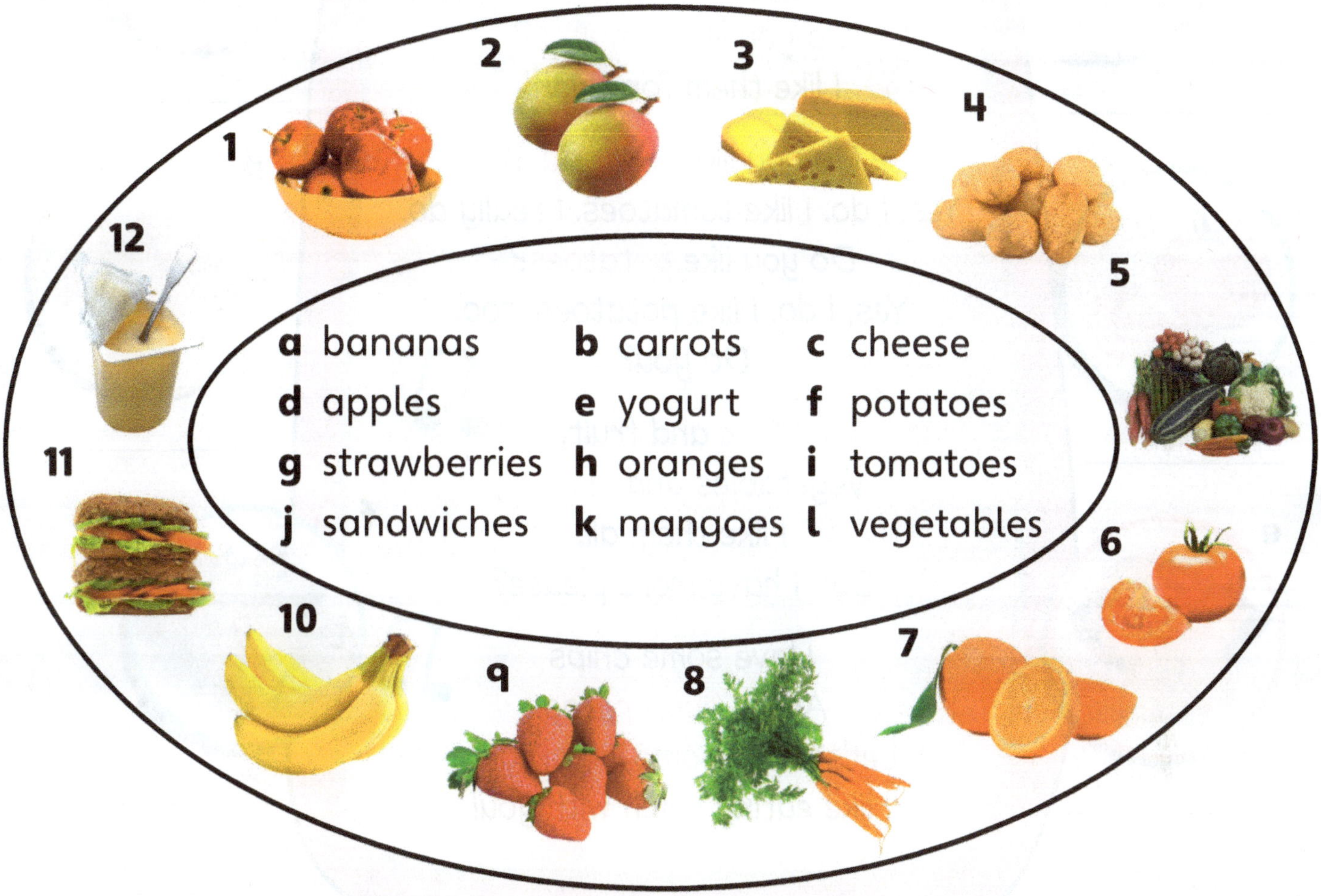

1
2
3
4
5
6
7
8
9
10
11
12

a bananas **b** carrots **c** cheese
d apples **e** yogurt **f** potatoes
g strawberries **h** oranges **i** tomatoes
j sandwiches **k** mangoes **l** vegetables

2 Look and write.

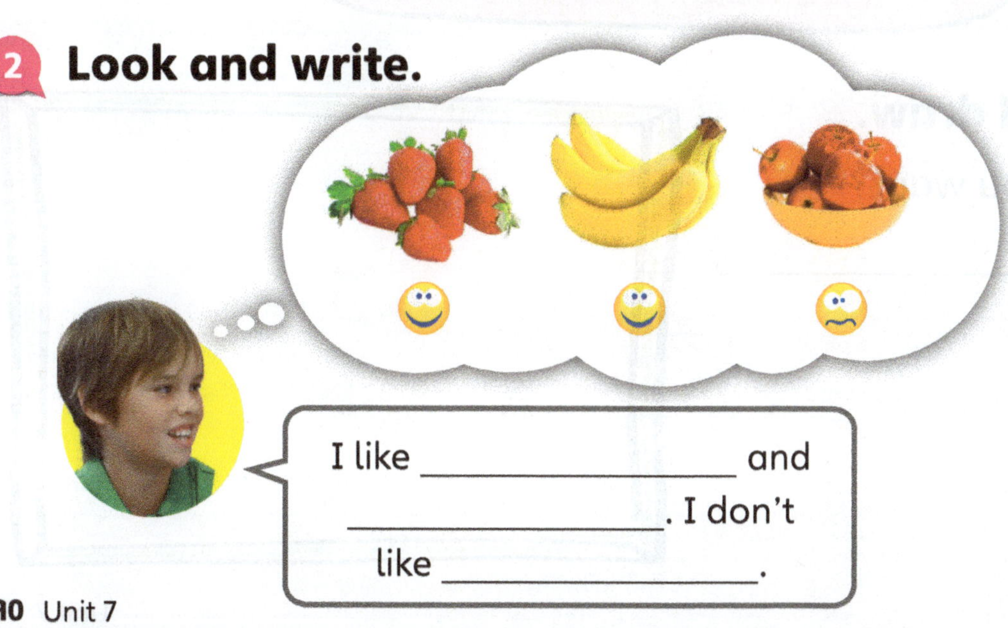

I like ________________ and ________________. I don't like ________________.

146

3 Listen and sing. Match and write.

a

____

b

____

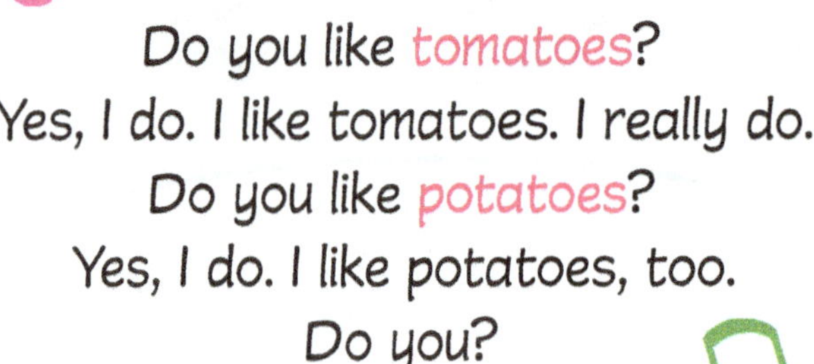

Let's Eat Lunch!

It's twelve o'clock.
Let's eat lunch.
Do you like bananas?
I like them for lunch!

Do you like tomatoes?
Yes, I do. I like tomatoes. I really do.
Do you like potatoes?
Yes, I do. I like potatoes, too.
Do you?

Meat and fruit,
Vegetables and snacks,
I like them all.
Can I have more please?

Have some chips
And a burger, too.
Let's share some ice cream.
I like eating lunch with you!

c

____

d

____

e

____

f

____

4 Write and draw.

What do you want?

I want ______________.

5 **Read. Then circle T for true and F for false.**

1	It's six o'clock.	T	F
2	Dan and Jamie want a snack.	T	F
3	Dan likes bananas.	T	F
4	Jamie doesn't like bananas.	T	F
5	Dan likes mangoes.	T	F

Circle the fruit.

mangoes bananas carrots oranges apples potatoes meat

6 What do you like? Listen and circle.

149

1 a  b 

2 a  b 

3 a  b 

4 a  b 

7 Look and write.

1  

I like ______________________

______________________.

I don't like ______________________.

2 

I like ______________________.

I don't like ______________________

______________________.

3 

I like ______________________

______________________.

I don't like ______________________.

4 

I like ______________________.

I don't like ______________________

______________________.

8 Look and circle.

1 

Do / **Does** she like strawberries?
Yes, she **do** / **does**.

2 

Do / **Does** he like tomatoes?
No, he **don't** / **doesn't**.

3 

Do / **Does** they like sandwiches?
Yes, they **do** / **does**.

4 

Do / **Does** they like cheese?
No, they **don't** / **doesn't**.

9 Match. Then write.

1 Do you like meat?	a 🙂 Yes, he ____________.
2 Do they like vegetables?	b 🙁 No, I ____________.
3 Does he like burgers?	c 🙂🙂 Yes, they ____________.

10 Are the snacks healthy or unhealthy? Put a ✓ or a ✗.

11 Read and write. Then listen and check.

152

fat healthy labels salt sugar unhealthy

Fruit and vegetables help us grow and keep us from getting sick. Some snacks are [1] ____________ because they have too much sugar, fat, or salt in them.

[2] ____________ in cookies and candy gives us energy, but it makes us fatter. It's bad for our teeth and can give us diabetes.

Too much fat also makes us fatter. Too much fat and salt can give us heart disease. Chocolate has a lot of [3] ____________ in it, and chips have a lot of [4] ____________ in them.

Always read the [5] ____________ on snacks and choose only [6] ____________ snacks.

12 Look at 11 and circle.

1 Too much **fruit / sugar** is unhealthy.

2 Cookies and candy give us **heart disease / energy**.

3 Too much sugar **keeps us from getting sick / makes us fatter**.

4 **Chocolate / Fruit** has a lot of fat in it.

5 **Chips / Cookies** can give us diabetes.

6 Healthy snacks **have / don't have** too much sugar, salt, or fat in them.

13 Read and write candy, cookies, chocolate, or chips.

1 There's too much salt in this snack. ____________

2 There's too much sugar in these snacks. ____________, ____________

3 There's too much fat in this snack. ____________

4 These snacks can give us diabetes. ____________, ____________

5 These snacks can give us heart disease. ____________, ____________

6 These snacks can make us fatter. ____________, ____________, ____________, ____________

Write about your favorite snack. Then circle.

My favorite snack is ____________________.

It's **healthy / unhealthy**.

14 Can you count it? Put a ✓ or a ✗.

a ☐

b ☐

c ☐

d ☐

e ☐

f ☐

g ☐

h ☐

15 Look at 14. Write a, an, or some.

1 __________ milk

2 __________ cookie

3 __________ juice

4 __________ apple

5 __________ cheese

6 __________ fruit

7 __________ burger

8 __________ chocolate

16 Read and match.

1 There are some

2 There's a

3 There's an

4 There's some

a banana on the table.

b chips on the plate.

c water in the glass.

d apple in the basket.

17 Look and write.

avocado kiwi fruit pineapple watermelon

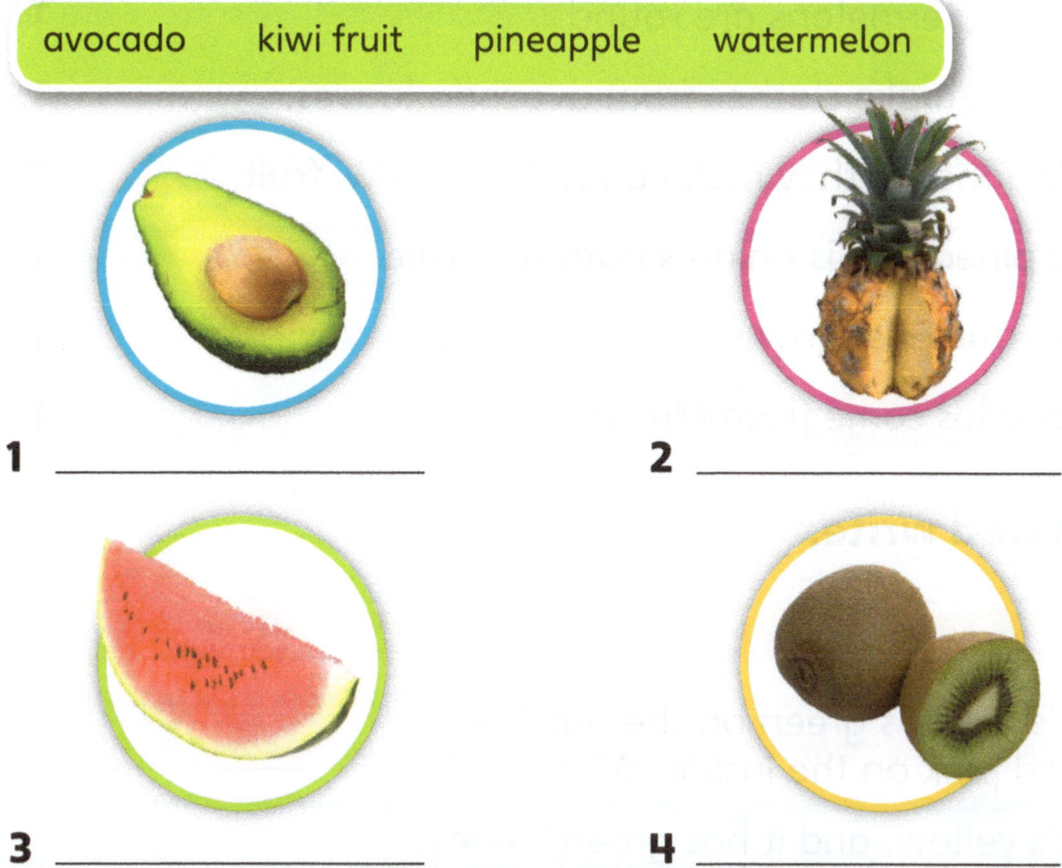

1 ____________ 2 ____________

3 ____________ 4 ____________

18 Read and circle. Then listen and check.

They come from Mexico but also from a lot of other countries. In Indonesia, people make [1] **candy / a drink** with avocado, milk, sugar, and sometimes chocolate.

They come from South Africa, Turkey, China, and Japan. In Japan, some watermelons are [2] **square / sweet**!

They come from South America and the Philippines. In the Philippines, people make [3] **clothes / skin** from pineapple leaves.

They're ugly outside but [4] **beautiful / national** inside. They come from China, but they now grow in many countries around the world.

19 Look at 18. Circle T for true and F for false.

1 Most watermelons are round. T F

2 You can make clothes from avocado leaves. T F

3 In Indonesia, they make a drink with kiwi fruit. T F

4 The pineapple is China's national fruit. T F

5 Watermelons grow in Turkey and South Africa. T F

6 Avocados come from Mexico. T F

20 Read and write.

Guess the fruit!

1 It's big. It's green on the outside and pink on the inside. What is it? ____________

2 It's yellow, and it has green leaves. What is it? ____________

3 It's green, and it has a very big seed inside. What is it? ____________

4 It's small and brown on the outside and green on the inside. What is it? ____________

THINK BIG

Draw your favorite fruit. Where does it come from?

____________ is my favorite fruit. It comes from ____________. It's ____________ and ____________.

Values | Choose healthy foods.

21 Look and circle.

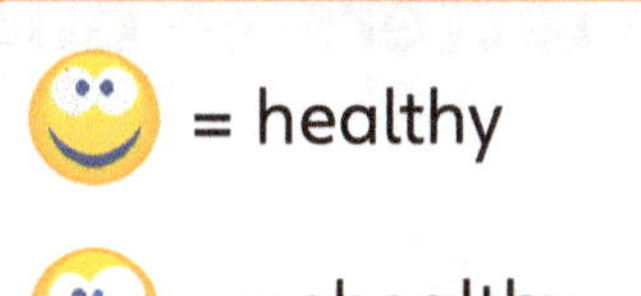

22 Find and write the sentences.

1 one | Just | please. | cookie,

____

2 thanks. | No | me, | chips | for

____

23 **Find and circle the letters ee and ie.**

24 **Read and circle the letters ee and ie.**

25 **Match the words with the same sounds.**

1 lie
2 see

a feet
b cried

162

26 **Listen and write the words. Then chant.**

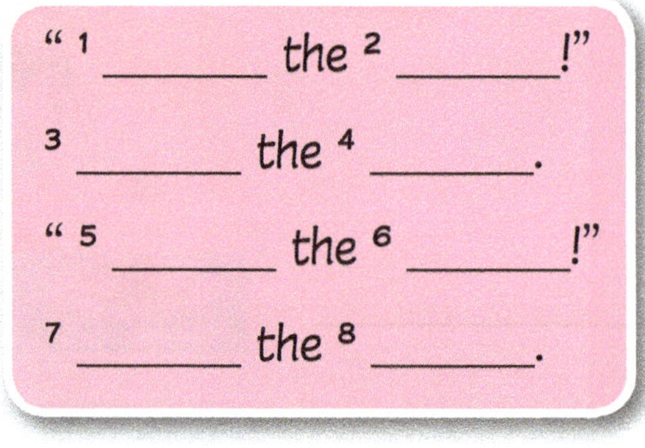

27 What do you like? Look and write five foods.

1 ______________________

2 ______________________

3 ______________________

4 ______________________

5 ______________________

28 Look and write.

1

Does she like bananas?

______________ .

2

He ____________ carrots.

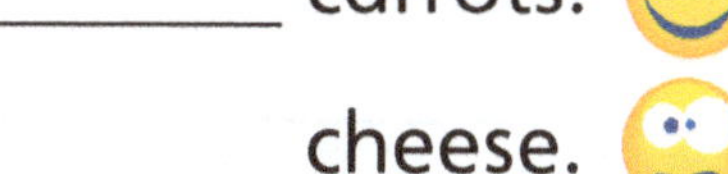

He ____________ cheese.

3

Does she like snacks?

______________ .

She ____________ meat.

4

They ____________ cheese.

They ____________ sandwiches.

29 Look and write.

Anna				
Ruben				
Mary				
You				

= like

= doesn't like

1 ____________ Anna ____________ tomatoes?

____

2 ____________ Ruben ____________ strawberries?

____

3 ____________ Mary ____________ potatoes?

____

4 ____________ Mary and Ruben ____________ burgers?

____

5 ____________ you ____________ burgers?

____

30 Read and circle.

1 Do you want **a** / **some** water?
2 There is **a** / **an** avocado tree in my garden.
3 Can I have **some** / **a** bananas, please?
4 I'm eating a burger and **a** / **some** chips.
5 There **is** / **are** some milk in the fridge.
6 There **is** / **are** two tomatoes on the table.

Wild Animals

1 Look and write.

cheetahs giraffes hippos kangaroos
monkeys polar bears zebras

ZOO

1 ______
2 ______
3 ______
4 ______
5 ______
6 ______
7 ______

2 Look and match.

1 crocodile 2 parrot 3 snake 4 peacock

a 
b 
c 
d 

168

3 Listen and sing. Write the words.

To the Zoo!

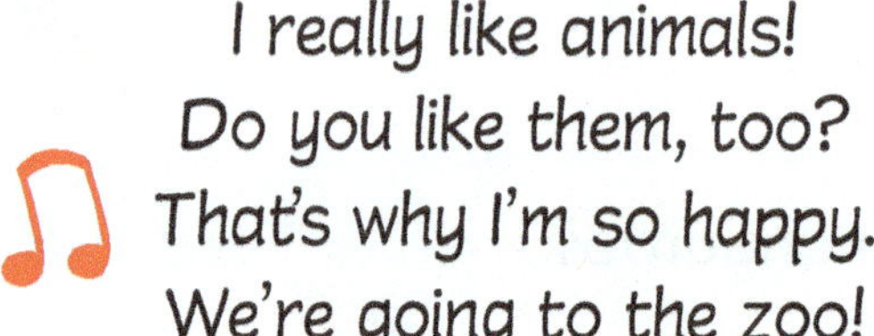

I really like animals!
Do you like them, too?
That's why I'm so happy.
We're going to the zoo!

A [1] ______________ can jump.
A [2] ______________ can jump, too.
Crocodiles can chase and swim.
And you, what can you do?

A [3] ______________ can't fly or jump up high.
An [4] ______________ can't climb trees.
Fish can't run, and hippos can't fly.
Come and see them.
Oh, yes, please!

Now it's time to say goodbye
To every animal here.
But we can come back
And see them every year!

kangaroo

elephant

monkey

polar bear

4 What animals do you like seeing at the zoo?

______________ ______________ ______________

______________ ______________ ______________

5 Read and circle.

1 **Monkeys** / **Hippos** can climb trees.

2 **Monkeys** / **Hippos** can eat a lot of food.

3 **Monkeys** / **Hippos** can jump.

4 **Monkeys** / **Hippos** have big mouths.

5 **Jamie** / **Jenny** can eat a lot.

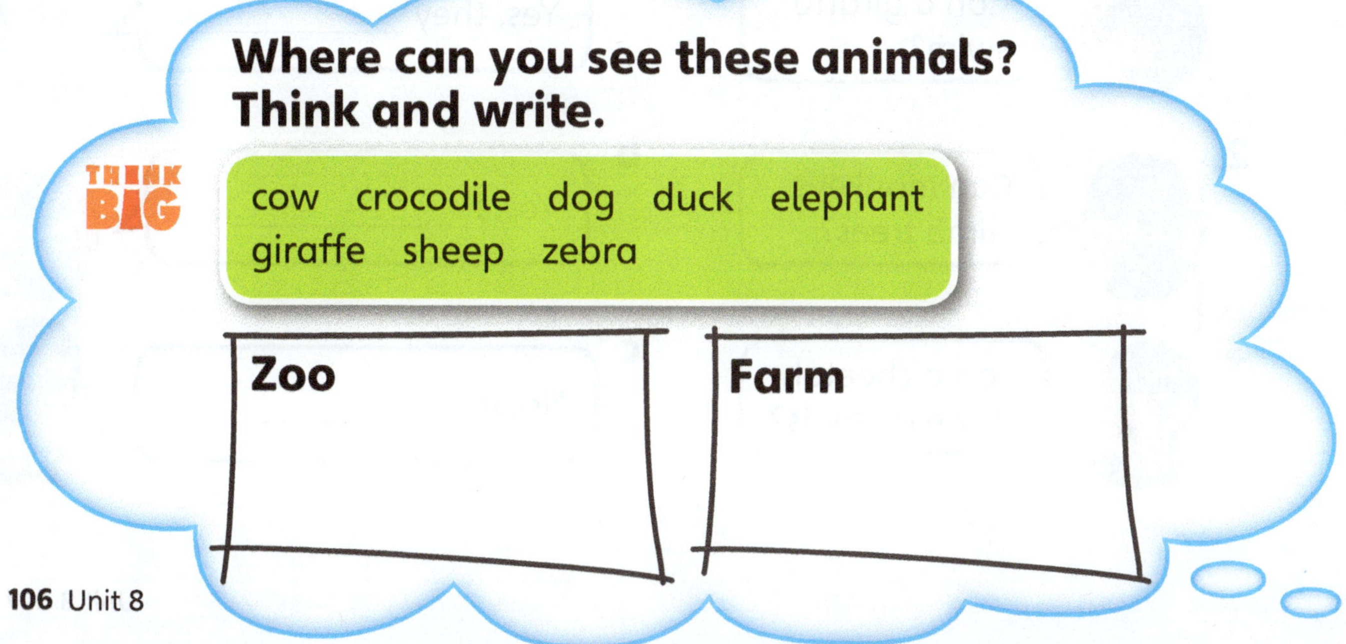

6 Read and answer. Follow the correct path to the zoo.

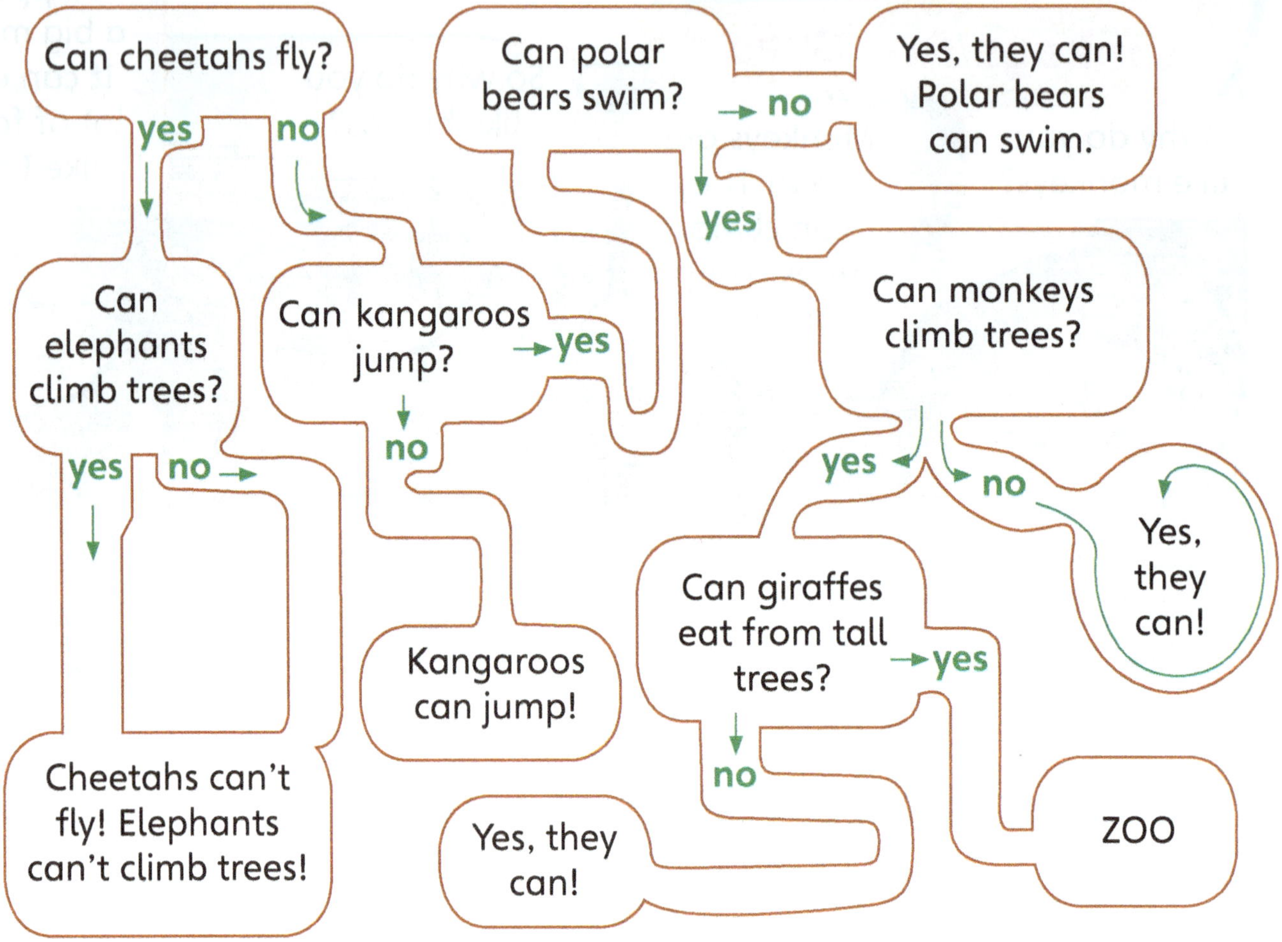

Can cheetahs fly? yes → Can elephants climb trees? / no → Can kangaroos jump?

Can elephants climb trees? yes → / no →

Cheetahs can't fly! Elephants can't climb trees!

Can kangaroos jump? yes → / no → Kangaroos can jump!

Can polar bears swim? no → Yes, they can! Polar bears can swim. / yes → Can monkeys climb trees?

Can monkeys climb trees? yes → Can giraffes eat from tall trees? / no → Yes, they can!

Can giraffes eat from tall trees? yes → ZOO / no → Yes, they can!

7 Match and write. Use can or can't.

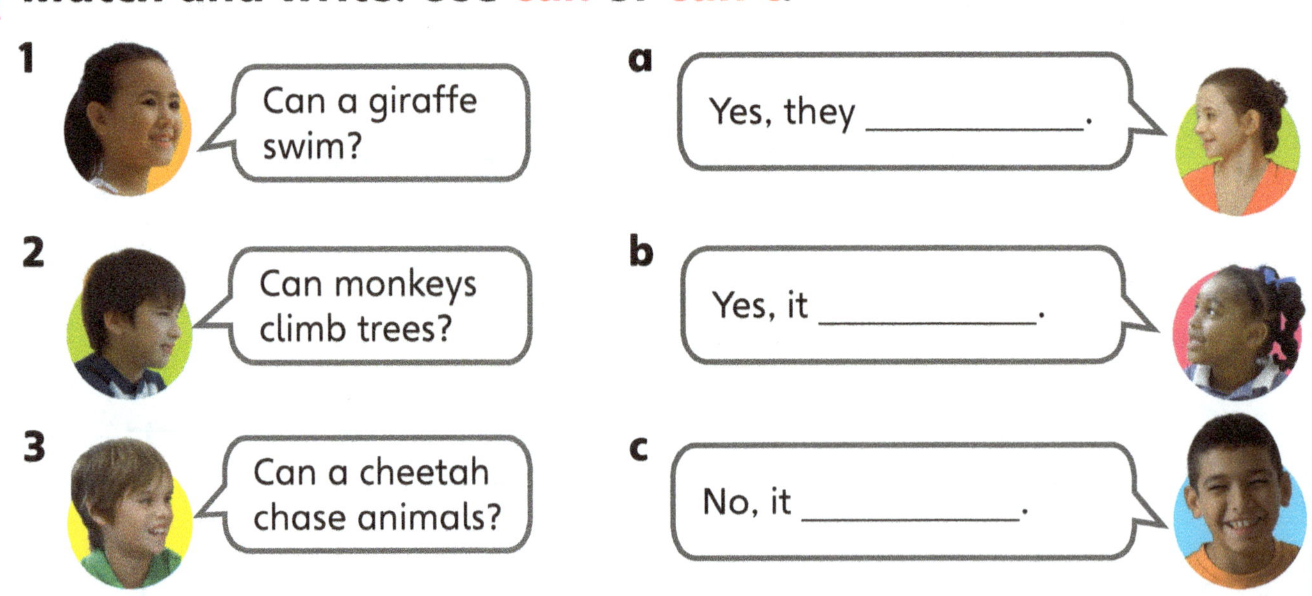

1 Can a giraffe swim?

2 Can monkeys climb trees?

3 Can a cheetah chase animals?

a Yes, they ____________.

b Yes, it ____________.

c No, it ____________.

8 **Look at the chart. Write questions and answers.**

	run	jump	climb trees	catch animals
1 giraffes	yes	no	no	no
2 polar bears	yes	yes	yes	yes
3 hippos	yes	no	no	no
4 cheetahs	yes	yes	yes	yes
5 zebras	yes	yes	no	no
6 kangaroos	no	yes	no	no

1 ______________________________ run?

_______________, they _______________.

2 ______________________________ jump?

_______________, they _______________.

3 ______________________________ climb trees?

_______________, they _______________.

4 ______________________________ catch animals?

_______________, they _______________.

5 ______________________________ run?

_______________, they _______________.

6 ______________________________ climb trees?

_______________, they _______________.

9 Read and complete.

desert forest jungle ocean

1 Tigers live in the ____________.

2 Fish live in the ____________.

3 A lizard lives in the ____________.

4 A deer lives in the ____________.

10 Listen, read, and match.

173

1 It's hot, and it rains a lot. Monkeys, birds, butterflies, and tigers live here.

2 It's cool and dark in the forest, and there are a lot of trees.

3 Lizards and snakes live here. There aren't many plants because it's very dry.

4 The ocean covers 71% of the planet. Many kinds of fish live in the ocean.

a About 6% of the planet is desert.

b Deer, raccoons, and foxes live here, too.

c Whales and seals also live in the salty water.

d The jungle covers only 2% of the planet, but 50% of all plants and animals live here.

11 Look at 10 and circle.

1 It's **dry** / **cool** in the desert.

2 It's **hot** / **dry** in the jungle.

3 The ocean covers **17%** / **71%** of the planet.

4 Colorful birds live in the **desert** / **jungle**.

5 There are a lot of trees and plants in the **desert** / **forest**.

12 Look and write.

1 ________________ live in ________________.

2 ________________ live in ________________.

3 ________________ live in ________________.

4 ________________ live in ________________.

THINK BIG **Circle the odd one out. Which animals live in oceans?**

fish lizard seal shark whale

13 Complete the table.

beautiful big blue brown cold long
new nice old pink small square

opinion	size/shape	age	color

14 Read and circle.

1 You have a **red nice** / **nice red** bike.

2 My grandpa is **a kind old** / **an old kind** man.

3 Is this your **blue new** / **new blue** scarf?

4 A kiwi fruit is a **funny brown** / **brown funny** fruit.

5 That's a **black beautiful** / **beautiful black** bird.

15 Look and write.

1 It's a ____________ ____________ monkey. (brown / small)

2 Those are ____________ ____________ birds. (red / big)

3 There are a lot of ____________ ____________ fish in the ocean. (beautiful / round)

4 Look at that ____________ ____________ watermelon! (pink / square)

5 I have a(n) ____________ ____________ desk. (old / nice)

16 Look and write.

koala llama snow monkey

1 ______________ 2 ______________ 3 ______________

176 17 Read and write. Then listen and check.

forest friendly gum tree jump sleep snowballs

Angela lives in Peru with her llama, Papi. Papi isn't wild. He's a [1] ______________ pet, and he can [2] ______________ high.

Kyoko lives in Japan. There are a lot of snow monkeys in the [3] ______________ near her home. They like to make [4] ______________.

Vincent lives in Australia. There's a koala in the [5] ______________ outside his window. Koalas are very slow. They [6] ______________ and eat a lot.

18 Look at 17 and circle.

1 Angela's llama **is / isn't** wild.

2 Papi can **make snowballs / jump**.

3 Snow monkeys live in **Kyoko's garden / the forest**.

4 They are **wild / friendly**.

5 The koala **is / isn't** a pet.

6 It sleeps a lot, **but / and** it eats a lot.

19 Look at 17. Write the countries.

1 Llamas come from ____________.

2 Snow monkeys come from ____________.

3 Koalas come from ____________.

THINK BIG

Draw and write about your favorite animal for the Outside My Window website.

This is a ____________. It comes from ____________.

It lives ________________________.

It ________________________.

It's my favorite animal because ________________________.

178

20 Look, listen, and write.

1 I like peacocks.
They're so ______________.

2 Monkeys are so
______________.

3 Giraffes are ______________.
Their necks are so long.

4 Elephants are very
______________.

21 Find and write the describing words.

1 ______________ z a a m n g i

2 ______________ a m s t r

3 ______________ f l u t i u e b a

4 ______________ o g n t s r

22 Find and circle the letters ou and ow.

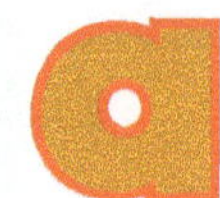

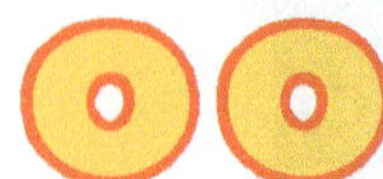

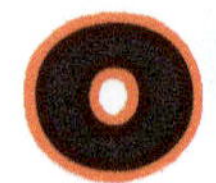

23 Read and circle the letters ou and ow.

1 you **2** owl **3** soup **4** cow

24 Match the words with the same sounds.

1 down **a** route
2 group **b** town

183
25 Listen and write the words. Then chant.

An [1]________ went
[2]________ to [3]________
To see a [4]________ of
[5]________ drinking
[6]________.

26 Look and write.

ACROSS →

3 

5 

6 

DOWN ↓

1 

2 

4 

27 Write. Then match questions and answers.

1 ____________ a monkey climb trees?

2 ____________ parrots fly?

3 ____________ a peacock swim?

4 ____________ snakes run?

a No, they ____________.

b Yes, it ____________.

c Yes, they ____________.

d No, it ____________.

28 Look and circle.

1 elephant / hippo **2 giraffe / crocodile** **3 lizard / snake**

29 Read and write.

deserts	forests	jungles	oceans

1 Foxes live in ____________.

2 Whales live in ____________.

3 Lizards live in ____________.

4 Monkeys live in __________.

30 Check (✓) the correct sentences.

1 Papi is an old friendly llama. ☐

2 Koalas are small slow animals. ☐

3 Snow monkeys are wild beautiful animals. ☐

4 An elephant is a big gray animal. ☐

5 My pet is a small black and white dog. ☐

Fun All Year

1 Number the months in order.

_____ **April**

SUN	MON	TUE	WED	THU	FRI	SAT
1	2	3	4	5	6	7
8	9	10	11	12	13	14
15	16	17	18	19	20	21
22	23	24	25	26	27	28
29	30					

_____ **January**

SUN	MON	TUE	WED	THU	FRI	SAT
1	2	3	4	5	6	7
8	9	10	11	12	13	14
15	16	17	18	19	20	21
22	23	24	25	26	27	28
29	30	31				

_____ **May**

SUN	MON	TUE	WED	THU	FRI	SAT
		1	2	3	4	5
6	7	8	9	10	11	12
13	14	15	16	17	18	19
20	21	22	23	24	25	26
27	28	29	30	31		

_____ **August**

SUN	MON	TUE	WED	THU	FRI	SAT
			1	2	3	4
5	6	7	8	9	10	11
12	13	14	15	16	17	18
19	20	21	22	23	24	25
26	27	28	29	30	31	

_____ **July**

SUN	MON	TUE	WED	THU	FRI	SAT
1	2	3	4	5	6	7
8	9	10	11	12	13	14
15	16	17	18	19	20	21
22	23	24	25	26	27	28
29	30	31				

_____ **November**

SUN	MON	TUE	WED	THU	FRI	SAT
				1	2	3
4	5	6	7	8	9	10
11	12	13	14	15	16	17
18	19	20	21	22	23	24
25	26	27	28	29	30	

_____ **December**

SUN	MON	TUE	WED	THU	FRI	SAT
						1
2	3	4	5	6	7	8
9	10	11	12	13	14	15
16	17	18	19	20	21	22
23	24	25	26	27	28	29
30	31					

_____ **June**

SUN	MON	TUE	WED	THU	FRI	SAT
					1	2
3	4	5	6	7	8	9
10	11	12	13	14	15	16
17	18	19	20	21	22	23
24	25	26	27	28	29	30

_____ **October**

SUN	MON	TUE	WED	THU	FRI	SAT
	1	2	3	4	5	6
7	8	9	10	11	12	13
14	15	16	17	18	19	20
21	22	23	24	25	26	27
28	29	30	31			

_____ **February**

SUN	MON	TUE	WED	THU	FRI	SAT
			1	2	3	4
5	6	7	8	9	10	11
12	13	14	15	16	17	18
19	20	21	22	23	24	25
26	27	28				

_____ **March**

SUN	MON	TUE	WED	THU	FRI	SAT
				1	2	3
4	5	6	7	8	9	10
11	12	13	14	15	16	17
18	19	20	21	22	23	24
25	26	27	28	29	30	31

_____ **September**

SUN	MON	TUE	WED	THU	FRI	SAT
						1
2	3	4	5	6	7	8
9	10	11	12	13	14	15
16	17	18	19	20	21	22
23	24	25	26	27	28	29
30						

2 Write the month.

1 This month has five letters.
This month is before April.

____

2 This month has six letters.
This month is after July.

____

3 This month has eight letters.
This month is between October and December.

____

189

3 Listen and chant. Then write.

4 What month do you like? Write. Then circle how many days it has.

____

S	M	T	W	T	F	S
		1	2	3	4	5
6	7	8	9	10	11	12
13	14	15	16	17	18	19
20	21	22	23	24	25	26
27	28	29	30	31		

5 Read and write.

1 Jenny's favorite month is ________.

2 Jenny ________ goes on vacation in December.

3 Dan ________ goes on vacation in the winter.

4 It's too ________.

What do you do in December?

I always ______________________ in December.

I never ______________________ in December.

6 Look at the calendar. Then write and circle.

June

Sun	Mon	Tues	Wed	Thur	Fri	Sat
				1	2	3
4	5	6	7	8	9	Visit Cousins 10
11	12	13	14	Sally's party 15	16	17
Father's Day 18	19	20	21	22	23	Beach 24
25	26	27	28	29	30	

1 Do you have a New Year's party in June?
No, I ____________. I **always** / **never** have a New Year's party in June.

2 What do you do in June?
I **always** / **never** visit my cousins in June.

3 What do you celebrate in June?
We **always** / **never** celebrate Father's Day in June.

4 Do you have Billy's party in June?
No, we ____________. We **always** / **never** have his party in June.

5 Do you go to the beach in June?
Yes, we ____________. We **always** / **never** go to the beach in June.

7 Answer about you. Write and circle.

Do you go on vacation in June?

____________, I ____________. I **always** / **never** go on vacation in June.

8 Look and write **always** or **never**.

Hi, I'm Julia. I always go ice-skating in the winter.

	winter	spring	summer	fall
always	go ice-skating	have a party	go to the beach	visit my cousins
never	ride my bike	go on vacation	go to school	celebrate New Year's

1 What does she do in the winter?

She ____________ rides her bike. She ____________ goes ice-skating.

2 What does she do in the spring?

She ____________ has a party. She ____________ goes on vacation.

3 What does she do in the summer?

She ____________ goes to the beach. She ____________ goes to school.

4 What does she do in the fall?

She ____________ celebrates New Year's. She ____________ visits her cousins.

9 Choose a season. Then write.

What do you do in the ____________________?

I always ____________________. I never ____________________.

10 Read and match for you.

In my country,

1 February and March are
2 May is
3 July and August are
4 September and October are

a in the spring.
b in the summer.
c in the fall.
d in the winter.

194 11 Listen, circle, and match.

1 On May Day, children in England hold **wishes** / **ribbons** and dance around a **tree** / **pole**.

2 In February and March, there are carnivals in Italy. People wear masks and throw small pieces of paper called **bamboo** / **confetti**.

3 The Mid-Autumn Festival in China happens when the **star** / **moon** is very big. Children wear **ribbons** / **costumes** and eat mooncakes.

4 In the summer, people in Japan celebrate Tanabata, the star festival. They **hang** / **wear** wishes on a bamboo **ribbon** / **wish** tree.

a

b

c

d

12 Look at 11 and match.

1 People celebrate May Day
2 On May Day, children dance
3 There are carnivals in Italy
4 At the carnival, children throw
5 At Mid-Autumn Festival, children eat
6 At Tanabata, people hang wishes

a on a bamboo tree.
b confetti.
c mooncakes.
d around a pole.
e in February and March.
f in the spring.

13 Look at 11. Write the countries.

1 In ____________, people throw confetti.
2 In ____________, people eat mooncakes.
3 In ____________, people celebrate the star festival.
4 In ____________, children put ribbons on a pole.

THINK BIG

What do people do at your favorite festival? Check (✓) and write.

wear masks ☐ eat special food ☐ dance ☐ make wishes ☐ throw paper ☐

My favorite festival is called ____________________.

People ______________________________

and ____________________________.

14 Read and match.

What's the weather like?

1 It's cold.

2 It's snowing.

3 It's hot.

4 It's sunny.

5 It's raining.

a 

b 

c 

d 

e  

15 Look and read. Circle T for true and F for false.

London, England	Paris, France	Mexico City, Mexico	New York, USA	Istanbul, Turkey	Tokyo, Japan	Shanghai, China	Rome, Italy

1 It's cold in London. T F

2 It's hot in Mexico City. T F

3 It's sunny and cold in Istanbul. T F

4 It isn't raining in Rome. T F

16 Look at 15 and write.

1 It's ____________ in Paris.

2 It's ____________ in New York.

3 It's ____________ and ____________ in Tokyo.

4 It's ____________ and ____________ in Shanghai.

17 Look at the pictures in 18 and match. Write 1–3.

soup ☐

grapes ☐

coal ☐

198

18 Listen, read, and match.

1 At midnight on New Year's Eve in Scotland, people hold hands and sing a special song. Then they visit their family and friends.

2 In Japan, people eat a special noodle soup on New Year's Eve for good luck.

3 In Spain, people eat twelve grapes at midnight. They eat one grape for each chime of the clock.

a People think that the grapes bring good luck. Then there are fireworks.

b Then they listen to a bell ring 108 times at midnight.

c The first person through the door gives a piece of coal for good luck.

19 Look at 18. Write Scotland, Japan, or Spain.

1 They listen to something. ____________

2 They hold hands. ____________

3 They eat fruit. ____________

4 They have fireworks. ____________

5 They eat soup. ____________

6 They visit people. ____________

20 Read and match.

1 How many grapes do they eat at midnight in Spain?

2 What happens after they eat the grapes?

3 How many times does a bell ring at midnight in Japan?

4 What do people in Scotland believe brings good luck on New Year's?

5 What is in the special New Year's soup in Japan?

a noodles

b 108

c fireworks

d 12

e a piece of coal

THINK BIG

What do you do on New Year's Eve?

On New Year's Eve, I ____________________

____

____________________________.

Values | Be active all year.

21 Read, look, and match.

1 In the spring, he rides his bike.

a 

2 In the summer, she likes to swim in the ocean.

b

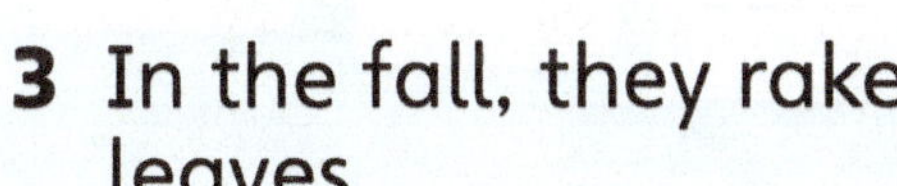

3 In the fall, they rake leaves.

c 

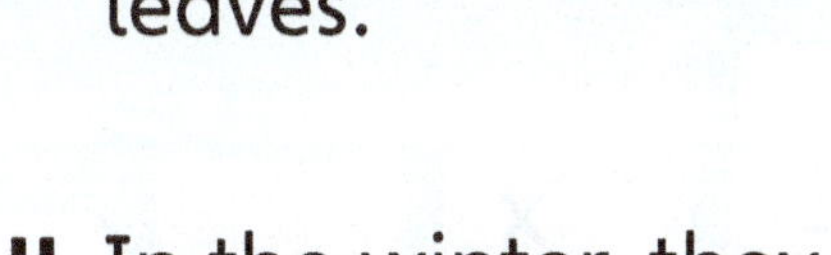

4 In the winter, they skate on ice.

d 

22 Find and write the words. Then match each season to the months in your country.

1 t n r e w i ______________

2 r p s g n i ______________

3 l a f l ______________

4 m r e u s m ______________

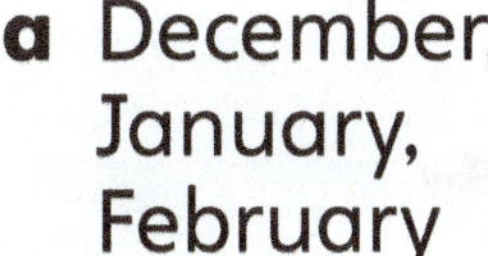

a December, January, February

b March, April, May

c June, July, August

d September, October, November

23 Write the alphabet in the correct order.

202 24 Listen and write the letters and words. Then chant.

A, B, C, 1____, E, 2____, G.
I can see an ant and a 3________.
What can you see?
H, I, 4____, K, L, 5____, N, O, 6____.
I can see a 7________ and some ink. What can you see?
Q, 8____, S, T, 9____, V.
I can see a 10________ and a snake.
What can you 11________?
W, 12____, Y, and 13____.
14________ yellow wolves and
a 15________ are what I see!

25 Follow the maze. Write the months in order.

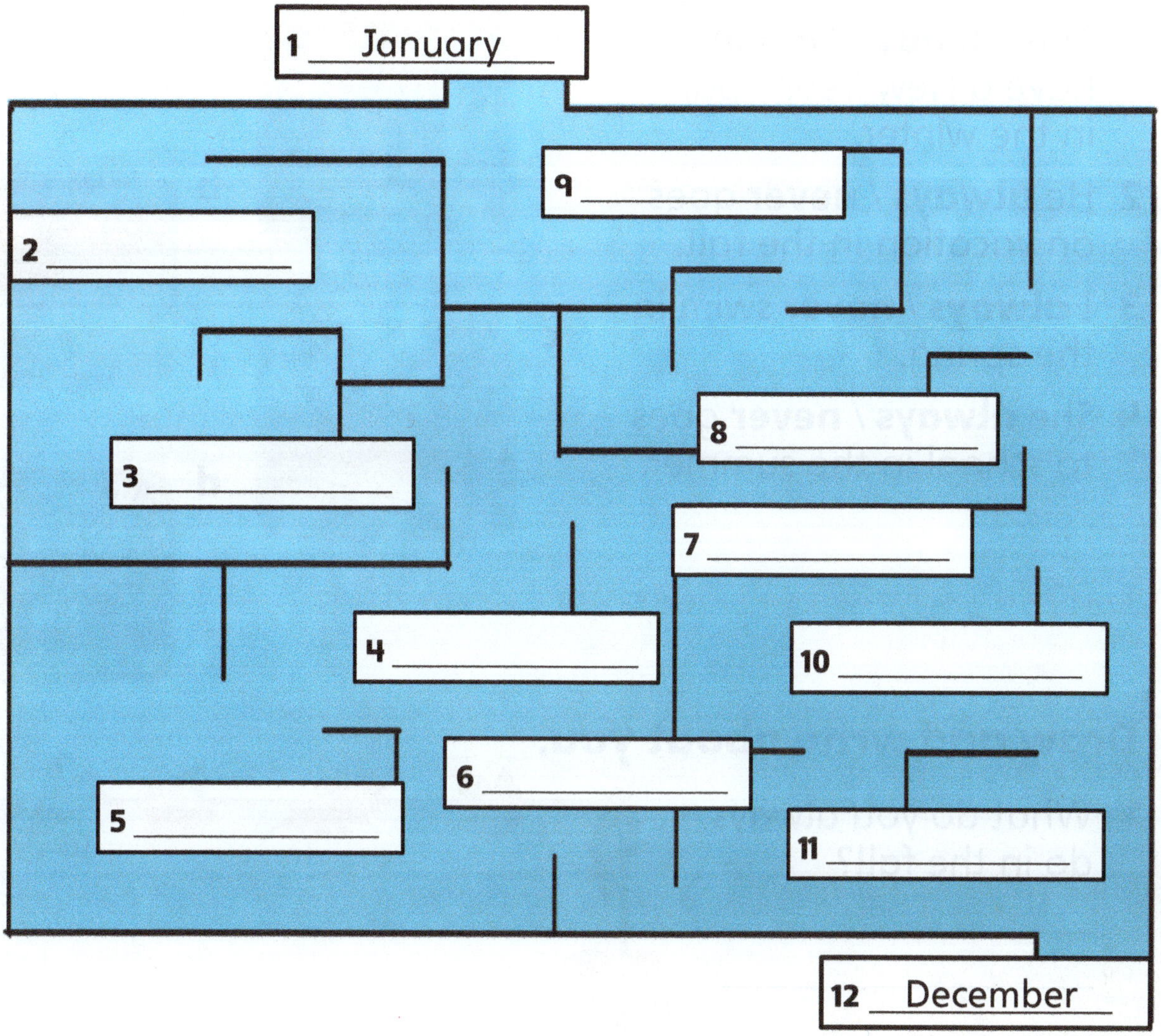

1 January

2 ______________

3 ______________

4 ______________

5 ______________

6 ______________

7 ______________

8 ______________

9 ______________

10 ______________

11 ______________

12 December

26 Complete the dialog.

always	Do	don't
never	What	

Maria: [1] __________ do you do in the winter?

Peter: We [2] __________ go ice-skating.

Maria: We always visit our cousins in the winter. We [3] __________ go ice-skating.

Peter: [4] __________ you go to the beach in the summer?

Maria: No, we don't. We [5] __________ go to the beach in the summer. We always go to the swimming pool and eat ice cream!

Listen and circle. Then match.

1 They **always** / **never** have a New Year's party in the winter.

2 He **always** / **never** goes on vacation in the fall.

3 I **always** / **never** swim in the spring.

4 She **always** / **never** goes to school in the summer.

a

b

c

d

28 Draw and write about you.

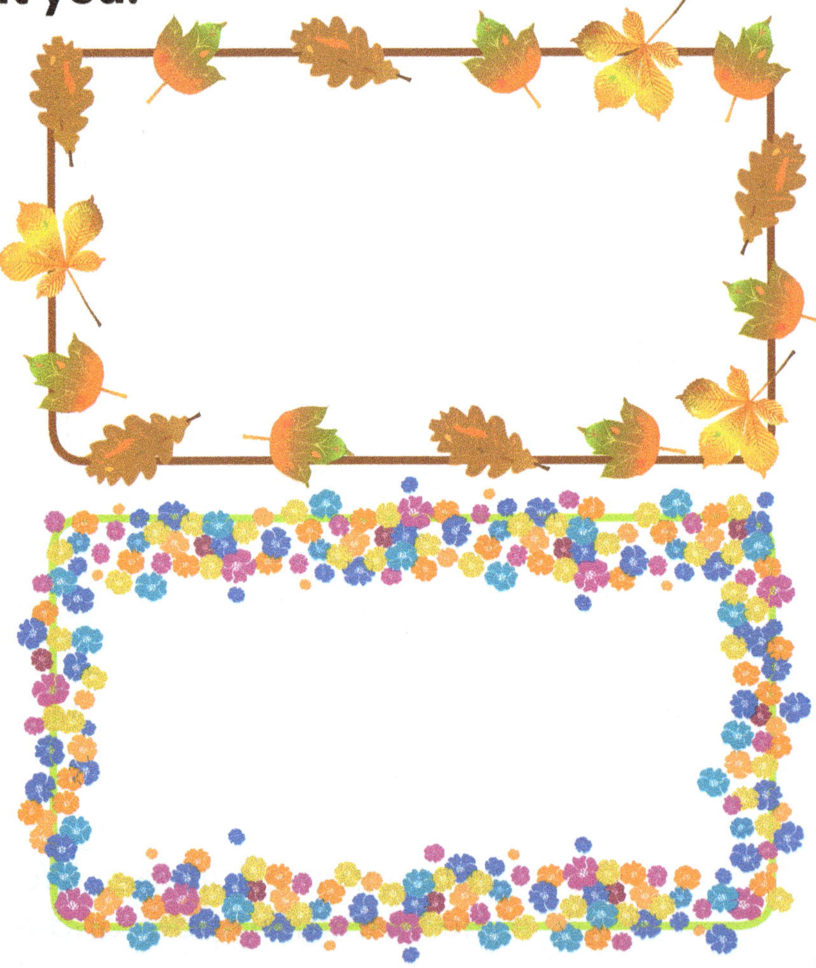

1 What do you always do in the fall?

____

____

What's the weather like?

____

____

2 What do you never do in the spring?

____

____

What's the weather like?

____

1 **Look, find, and number.**

2 **Look at 1 and write. Add one food word, one animal word, and one month word.**

3 **Look at the table and circle one food in red:**

What do you like eating for lunch?

4 **Look at the table and circle one food in blue:**

What do you never eat for lunch?

5 **Think, look, and circle in green.**

There's a hat on an elephant. That's silly. What other silly things can you see?

FOOD

1 carrots
2 cheese
3 bananas
____

ANIMALS
4 zebra
5 elephant
6 giraffe
MONTHS
7 summer month
8 winter month
9 fall month

What's he/she **doing**?	He'**s**/She'**s** **writing**.
What **are** they **doing**?	They'**re** **gluing**.

1 Circle the correct form of the verb. Then match.

1 What **is** / **are** he doing?
2 What **is** / **are** they doing?
3 What **is** / **are** she doing?

a She's coloring.
b They're watching a DVD.
c He's counting.

How many pictures are there?	**There's** one picture.
How many books are there?	**There are** three books.

2 Look and write. Use There's or There are.

1 ____________________ one teacher.
2 ____________________ one book.
3 ____________________ three pupils.

What **does** he/she **like doing**?	He/She **likes skateboarding**.
What **do** they **like doing**?	They **like flying kites**.

1 Circle the correct form of the verb.

1 What **do / does** he like doing?

He **like / likes** playing tennis.

2 What **do / does** they like doing?

They **like / likes** climbing trees.

3 What **do / does** she like doing?

She **like / likes** doing gymnastics.

2 Look and write the question. Then write the answer.

listen use

1 

What ________________ doing?

He ________________ the computer.

2 

What ________________ doing?

They ____________________________.

Where's the TV?	**It's** on the table.
Where **are** the chairs?	**They're** in the living room.

1 Look. Write Where's or Where are.

1 __________ the keys?
2 __________ the phone?
3 __________ the soccer ball?
4 __________ the skates?

2 Look at 1. Answer the questions.

1 __________ in the bedroom.
2 __________ on the bed.
3 __________ in the bath.
4 __________ next to the chair.

My mom**'s** phone is on the dresser.	Ben**'s** keys are on the table.

3 Circle the correct word.

1 Where are **Mom / Mom's** keys?

2 My **cousins / cousin's** are riding their bikes.

3 **Emily / Emily's** bedroom is next to the bathroom.

4 **Joes / Joe's** clothes are in the cupboard.

I/We/They/You **want to** send a letter.	He/She **wants to** go to the bank.

1 Circle the correct form of the verb.

1 I **want** / **wants** to buy a book.

2 My aunt and uncle **want** / **wants** to go to a computer store.

3 Julia **want** / **wants** to send a letter.

4 He **want** / **wants** to eat.

Is there a post office near here?	Yes, **there is.**
Is there a bank on Elm Street?	No, **there isn't.**

2 Look and write.

1 Is there a bookstore on High Street?

____

2 Is there a computer store on River Street?

____

3 ____________________ a movie theater near the train station?

____

4 Let's eat. ____________________ a restaurant near here?

Yes, ____________________

What **do** you **want to be**?	I **want to be** an actor.
What **does** he/she **want to be**?	He/She **wants to be** a doctor.

1 Look and write.

1

What does he want to be?

He ______________________.

2

What does she want to be?

She ______________________.

3

______________________?

She wants to be a pilot.

4

______________________?

He wants to be a chef.

5

______________________?

He ______________________.

6

What do you want to be?

____

When **does** he/she **get up**?	He/She **gets up** at 6:00.
When **do** you/they **go to** bed?	I/They **go to** bed at 8:00.
When **does** the movie **start**?	It **starts** at 7:00.

1 Look and match. Then write the questions and answers.

1 When

2 When

	they go out?
do	she get up?
does	she go to bed?
	school finish?

3 When

4 When

1 ____________________________________?

____

2 ____________________________________?

____

3 ____________________________________?

____

4 ____________________________________?

____

Do you **like** fruit?	Yes, I **do**. I like apples and bananas. No, I **don't**. I like cheese.
Do they **like** vegetables?	Yes, they **do**. They like carrots and potatoes. No, they **don't**. They like fruit.
Does he/she **like** fruit?	Yes, he/she **does**. He/She likes mangoes and oranges. No, he/she **doesn't**. He/She likes yogurt.

1 Circle the correct form of the verb.

1 **Do / Does** she like meat?
No, she **don't / doesn't**. She likes sandwiches.

2 **Do / Does** they like snacks?
Yes, they **do / does**.

3 **Do / Does** she like cheese?
Yes, she **do / does**.

4 **Do / Does** they like tomatoes?
No, they **don't / doesn't**. They like potatoes.

5 **Do / Does** you like strawberries?
Yes, I **do / does**. I love strawberries!

2 Look and write the questions and answers.

1 you	bananas	☹
2 Emma	oranges	☹
3 Sue and Hugo	vegetables	☺

1 ____________ you ____________ bananas? ____________

2 ____________ she ____________ oranges? ____________

3 ____________ they ____________ vegetables? ____________

Can a kangaroo jump?	Yes, it **can**.	**Can** a snake jump?	No, it **can't**.
Can kangaroos jump?	Yes, they **can**.	**Can** snakes jump?	No, they **can't**.

1 Read. Circle T for true and F for false.

1 Cheetahs can run. T F

2 A giraffe can fly. T F

3 A polar bear can jump. T F

4 An elephant can eat meat. T F

5 Hippos can climb trees. T F

6 Kangaroos can swim. T F

2 Look at 1. Correct the false sentences. Use can't.

1 ____________________

2 ____________________

3 ____________________

4 ____________________

3 Write the questions. Use the words. Then write the answer.

chase fly talk write

1 Can a cheetah ________ a zebra? Yes, ____________.

2 ________ a cheetah ________? No, ____________.

3 ________ cheetahs ________? No, ____________.

4 ________ cheetahs ________ their name? No, ____________.

What does he/she do in January?	He/She **always** has a New Year's party in January.
Do you go on vacation in the winter?	No, I/we don't. I/We **never** go on vacation in the winter.

1 Answer the questions about you. Circle the words.

1 Do you do homework at six o'clock?
Yes / **No**. I **always** / **never** do homework at six o'clock.

2 Does your father like reading books?
Yes / **No**. He **always** / **never** reads books.

3 Do you like playing games at school?
Yes / **No**. I **always** / **never** play games at school.

4 Does your family watch DVDs on TV?
Yes / **No**. We **always** / **never** watch DVDs.

5 Does your mom eat meat?
Yes / **No**. She **always** / **never** eats meat.

2 Look at the calendar. Write always or never.

Anna: What does he do in January?

Bill: He ____________ celebrates New Year's Day.

Anna: Does he celebrate New Year's in February, too?

Bill: No. He ____________ celebrates New Year's in February! That's silly.

January						
Sun	Mon	Tues	Wed	Thu	Fri	Sat
1 New Year's Day	2	3	4	5	6	7
8	9	10	11	12	13	14
15	16	17	18	19	20	21
22	23	24	25	26	27	28
29	30	31				

Write these words in your own language.

Unit 1	SB Page
classroom	4
coloring	4
counting	4
cutting	4
gluing	4
listening	4
playing a game	4
using the computer	4
watching a DVD	4
writing	4
a hundred	10
equals	10
minus	10
plus	10
take turns	16
bath	17
both	17
crocodile	17
math	17
mouth	17
path	17
teeth	17
then	17
thin	17
with	17
My favorite word:	

Unit 2	SB Page
climbing trees	20
doing gymnastics	20
flying kites	20
ice-skating	20
playing tennis	20
playing volleyball	20
riding my bike	20
skateboarding	20
like	21
love	21
playground	21
running	21
swing	21
together	22
team	23
bones	26
kick	26
muscles	26
take care of	26
throw	26
each side	32
helmet	32
in front of	32
knee pads	32
safely	32
slide	32
seesaw	32
bang	33
bank	33
ink	33
king	33
ring	33
sink	33
wing	33
My favorite word:	

Unit 3	SB Page
bathroom	36
bed	36
bedroom	36
chair	36
closet	36
couch	36
dresser	36
DVD player	36
fridge	36
kitchen	36
lamp	36
living room	36
oven	36
table	36
TV	36
behind	37

Word	Page
glasses	37
in	37
keys	37
on	37
put on	37
aunt	38
cousin	38
uncle	38
quiet	39
between	40
next to	40
under	40
phone	41
new	42
old	42
wheel	42
dirty	48
dishes	48
neat	48
toy box	48
washing machine	48
cook	49
cool	49
moon	49
zoo	49
My favorite word:	

Unit 4	SB Page
bank	58
bookstore	58
bus stop	58
computer store	58
gas station	58
movie theater	58
post office	58
restaurant	58
shopping mall	58
supermarket	58
town	58
train station	58
buy	59
eat	59
far	59
letter	59
map	59
near	59
send	59
first	60
hungry	60
wallet	61
movie	62
boat	64
go to school by	64
train	64
cross the street	70
last	70
left	70
pedestrian crossing	70
right	70
second	70
wait	70
drive	71
nail	71
oak	71
rain	71
sail	71
soap	71
tail	71
wear	71
My favorite word:	

Unit 5	SB Page
actor	74
artist	74
athlete	74
chef	74
dancer	74
doctor	74
dream job	74
pilot	74
singer	74
teacher	74
vet	74
writer	74
farmer	80
hairdresser	80

nurse	80
science	82
park ranger	85
protect	85
art	86
music	86
set goals	86
study hard	86
My favorite word:	

Unit 6	**SB Page**
o'clock	90
do my homework	91
evening	91
get dressed	91
get up	91
go out	91
go to bed	91
sleep	91
start school	91
stay in bed	91
watch	91
come back	92
in the afternoon	92
boring	93
finish school	94
cup	96
hourglass	96
sand	96
shadow	96
sundial	96
tell time	96
use	96
work	96
early	102
on time	102
quickly	102
ready	102
chin	103
chop	103
rich	103
ship	103
witch	103
My favorite word:	

Unit 7	**SB Page**
apples	112
bananas	112
burger	112
carrots	112
cheese	112
mangoes	112
meat	112
oranges	112
potatoes	112
sandwiches	112
snack	112
strawberries	112
tomatoes	112
vegetables	112
yogurt	112
fries	113
fruit	113
ice cream	113
share	113
pie	115
disease	118
fat	118
healthy	118
heart	118
salt	118
sugar	118
watermelon	122
avocado	123
kiwi	123
pineapple	123
popular	123
chocolate	123
bee	125
cried	125
flies	125
lie	125
sheep	125
tie	125
My favorite word:	

Wordlist

Unit 8	SB Page
cheetah	128
elephant	128
giraffe	128
hippo	128
kangaroo	128
monkey	128
parrot	128
peacock	128
polar bear	128
snake	128
wild	128
zebra	128
chase	129
at night	132
cold	134
colorful	134
dark	134
deer	134
desert	134
fox	134
jungle	134
lizard	134
plants	134
ocean	134
raccoon	134
seal	134
whale	134
amazing	136
appreciate	140
beautiful	140
smart	140
strong	140
clown	141
owl	141
soup	141
toucan	141

My favorite word: ______

Unit 9	SB Page
April	144
August	144
December	144
February	144
January	144
July	144
June	144
March	144
May	144
November	144
October	144
September	144
excited	145
month	145
winter	146
summer	148
spring	150
wish	150
good luck	154
midnight	154
ring	155
fall	156
ant	157
bat	157
rat	157

My favorite word: ______

ENGLISH
AROUND ME

Paste or draw things with English words.

MOVIE TICKET

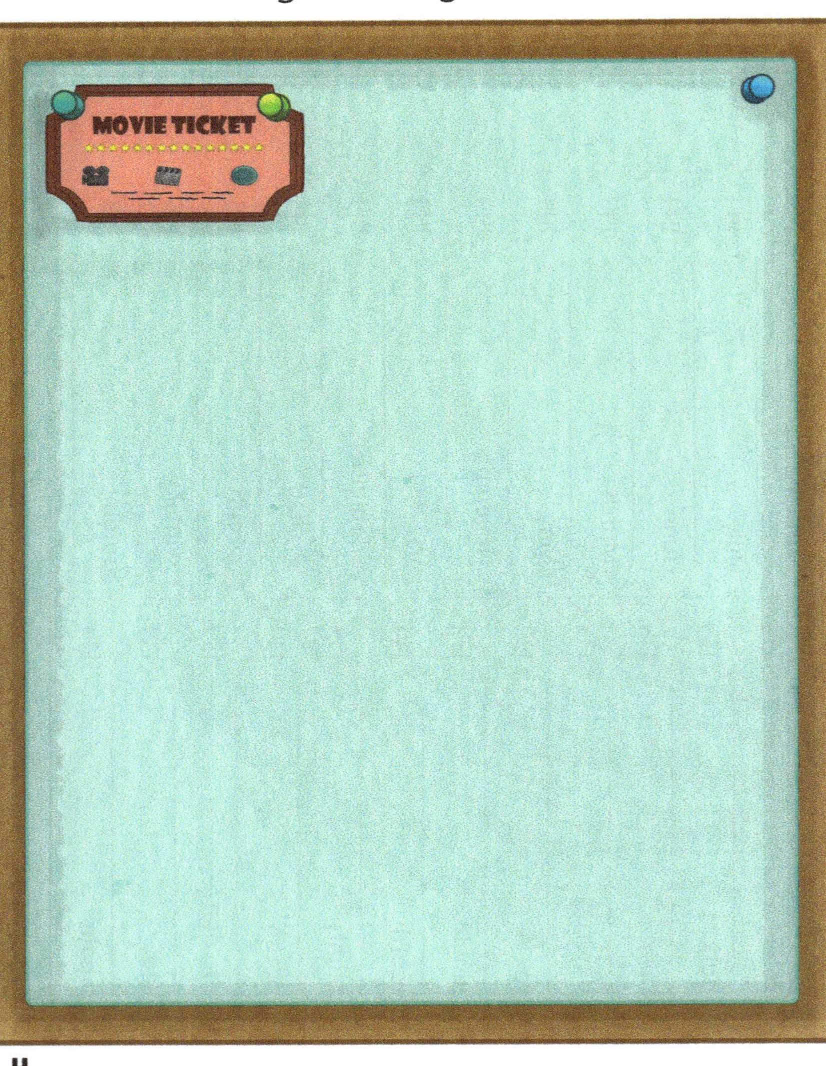

FOLD

Workbook 2

My BIG ENGLISH World

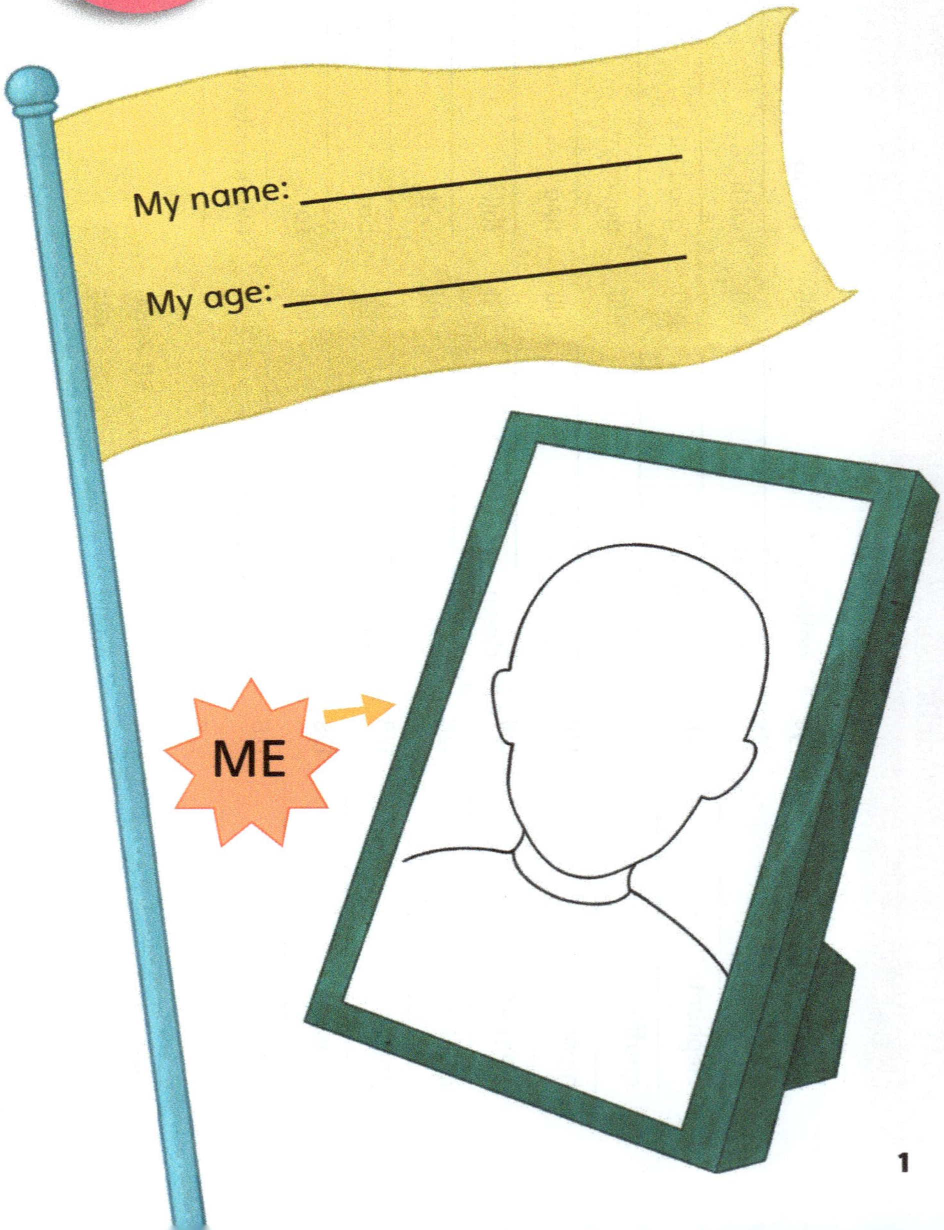
My name: ______
My age: ______
ME

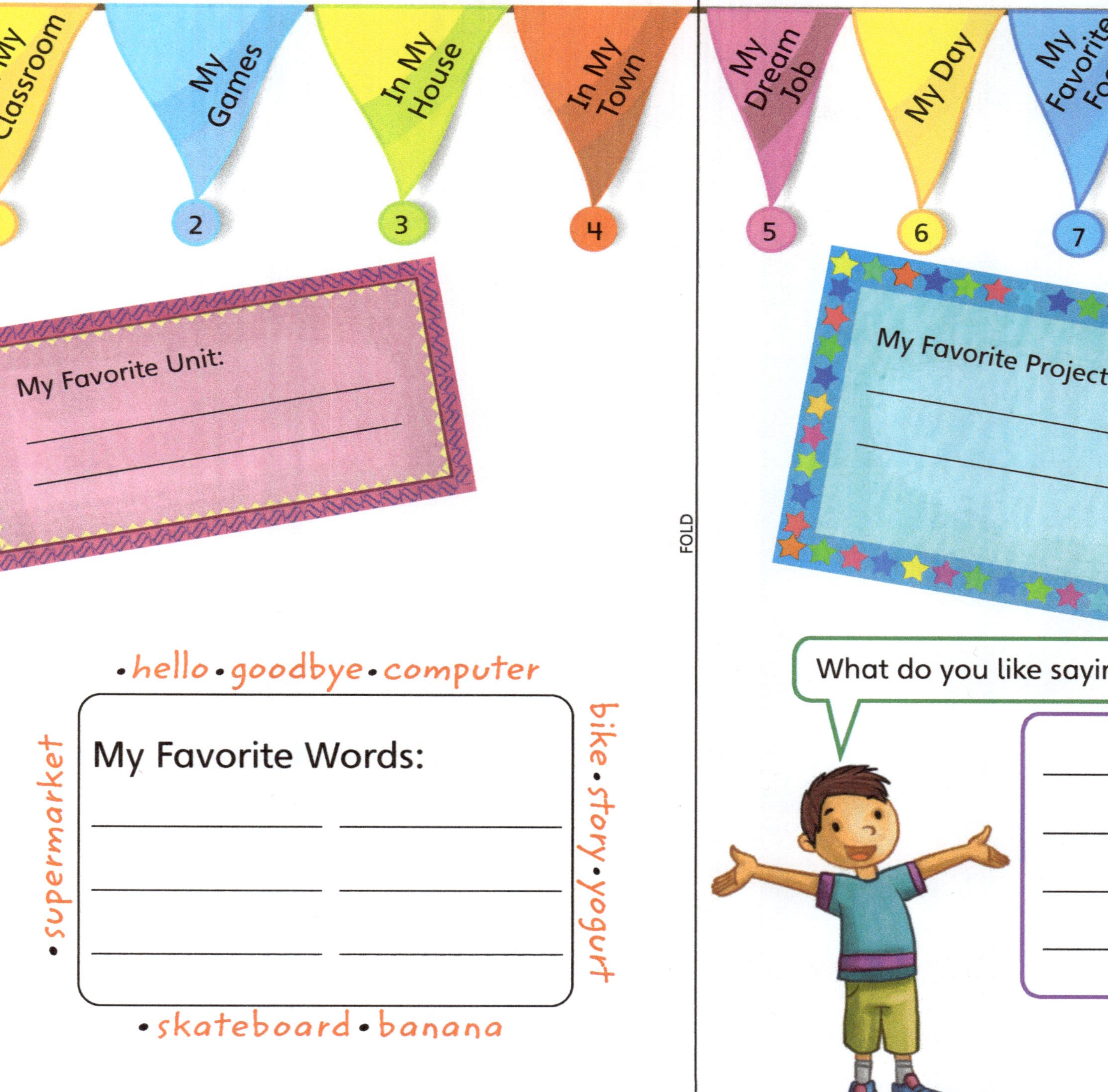

•hello •goodbye •computer

My Favorite Words:

•supermarket

•bike •story •yogurt

•skateboard •banana